Kitchen Keepsakes
By Request

Bonnie Welch & Deanna White

Illustrated by
Pam Hake

Published by Kitchen Keepsakes
39265 Co. Rd. 45-49
Kiowa, CO 80117
(303) 688-6538
or
(719) 347-2904

For ordering information, write or call:

Kitchen Keepsakes
39265 Co. Rd. 45-49
Kiowa, CO 80117
(303) 688-6538

or

Kitchen Keepsakes
19137 Rd. 69
Calhan, CO 80808
(719) 347-2904

March, 1993   First Printing
March, 1994   Second Printing
July, 1995   Third Printing

Printed in the USA by

WIMMER
The Wimmer Companies, Inc.
Memphis • Dallas

INTRODUCTION

In the nine years since we first published **Kitchen Keepsakes**, the response to our "cookbook project" has been overwhelming and most gratifying. The sale of over 100,000 copies of **Kitchen Keepsakes**, and **More Kitchen Keepsakes**, has shown us that there are indeed many who still enjoy the old-fashioned goodness of home cooking.

In the last several years we've had many requests from our readers for a third edition. We thought it would be a wonderful idea to tap the resources of our fellow home cooks and incorporate their family favorites, along with ours, into another cookbook. Their requests for a new cookbook, and our request to share recipes combined to create **Kitchen Keepsakes By Request**. This cookbook is truly a continuation of what we started, but it is more than that since the recipes gathered, tested, and included in this cookbook come from all over the nation and represent a variety of regional flavors.

This new treasury is full of over 450 down-home recipes that we kitchen-tested and edited for clarity. They are easy to prepare, call for recognizable and inexpensive ingredients, and are all delicious. We have, as always, included some menu suggestions, freezing and quick preparation ideas, and in some instances, alternatives or substitutions for lighter cooking.

Much has changed since those days nine years ago when **Kitchen Keepsakes** was first created. Our children, toddlers then, are now adolescents, and we have a different, though no less hectic, lifestyle. Our involvement in school activities, sports, 4-H livestock shows, cutting horse shows, and our ranching operations has made our time at home a precious commodity.

But despite these changes, one thing has remained constant…the pleasure we find in cooking a delicious, satisfying meal for our families and friends. In this age of fast food and take-home dinners, we continue to find that those meals made and eaten at home are still the best!

So in the tradition of good home cooking, and in hopes that we have added to your collection of keepsakes, we offer you **Kitchen Keepsakes By Request**.

DEDICATION

We dedicate this cookbook to our husbands and children:

John Welch	Jim White
Bob Welch	Tanya White
Andy Welch	Linda White
Wesley Welch	Will White

They have become our expert panel of "taste testers", endured countless trips to the printer, hauled hundreds of boxes of cookbooks, supported our decisions and indecision, and encouraged us to try it one more time. We love them.

IN APPRECIATION

The following people were vital to the creation of this cookbook. They generously shared their favorite recipes with us, making this cookbook a sampling of America's keepsakes. We sincerely thank them for their response, their patience, and their support of our endeavor.

Keith Arbogast, Boulder, CO
Betty Ardito, Monroe, LA
Colleen Austin, Kiowa, CO
Pattie Becker, Kiowa, CO
Karla Blach, Yuma, CO
Leslie Blanchard, Fullerton, CA
Suzie Bohleen, Wilsall, MT
Nancy Boykin, Woodbridge, VA
Kendra Brown, Sacramento, CA
Talley Brown,
    Colorado Springs, CO
Kathleen Budd, Franktown, CO
Betty Carter, Kingston, OH
Nancy Clawson, Gillette, WY
Jane Clepper, Austin, TX
Janice Collier, Buellton, CA
Dee Cornforth, Alberta, Canada
Laurie Cornforth, Alberta, Canada
Mary Cushing, Exton, PA
Helen Daly, Wheat Ridge, CO
Carol Daughenbaugh,
    San Bernardino, CA
Bill & Luella Deibel, Aurora, CO
Vicki Douglas, Fremont, CA
Pearl Eiker, Wheeling, IL
Polly Everett, Kiowa, CO
Karen Filip, Deer Field, IL
Mary Findling, Clackamas, OR
Debbie Ford, Canadian, TX
Pearl Fox, Milwaukee, OR
Susie Foy, Midland, TX
Christine Francis, Lusk, WY
Marjorie Freeman, Fullerton, CA
Bonnie Frihauf, Yuma, CO
Jane Furche, Ruidoso, NM
Sandy Gabel, Kersey, CO
Shannon Gabel, Broomfield, CO
Vicki Gabel, Broomfield, CO
Jerri Gallagher, Littleton, CO
Sherida Galley, Willow Park, TX
Gerilyn Glover, Calhan, CO
Joanie Graham, Longmont, CO

Willie Mae Graham, Macon, MS
Gayle Greenwood, Emerson, IA
Jan Hatfield, Monroeville, PA
Suzie Hawes, Englewood, CO
Meridee Hahn, Elbert, CO
Noanie Hepp, Longmont, CO
Betty Herzberg, Denver, CO
Paul Hicks, Ft. Worth, TX
Millie Huhman, New York, NY
Ruth Jackson, Broomfield, CO
Evelyn Johnson, Minot, ND
Polly Johnson, Kit Carson, CO
Sandra Johnson, Stanberry, MO
Susan Jones, Stow, OH
Marinan Keeling, Pleasanton, TX
Casey Kelley, Elizabeth, CO
Sid Kelsey, Pompey's Point, MT
Helen Klinger, Sussex, WI
Patty Koch, Duncanville, TX
Nancy Kuhn, Berne, IN
Ann Langenderfer, St. Peters, MO
Carol LaPerriere, Calhan, CO
Genny Lee, Norwalk, OH
Mary Jo Lewan, Longmont, CO
Mildred Little, Calhan, CO
Nancy Manson, Fargo, ND
Frances Matthews, Midland, TX
Donna Marrs, Kiowa, CO
Jo McClellan, Kirksville, MO
Sharon Miller, Kiowa, CO
Wilma Miller, Kiowa, CO
Dorsey Mojden, Hinsdale, IL
Ruth Morris, Newton, NC
Loretta Mulert, Saratoga, CA
Anna Nagy, Lincoln Park, MI
Donna Nichols, Max, NE
Joan Nudera,
    Colorado Springs, CO
Elaine Ohlman, Franktown, CO
Carrie Oquendo, Palmdale, CA
Linda Orth, Melrose, MN
Esther Pfannenstiel, Billings, MO

Donna Phillips, Pueblo, CO
Sherri Platt, Longmont, CO
Marion Potter, Stevensville, MT
Jeanne Pratt, Haverhill, MA
Donalee Price, Torrance, CA
Mrs. Barry Rankin, Lexington, KY
Helen Roane, Williamstown, NC
Jeannine Roettenbacher,
    Denver, CO
Betty Rotenbery, Aurora, CO
Grace Sayler, Wheat Ridge, CO
Lisa Saxton, Yuma, Co
Pat Schalla, Calhan, CO
Barbara Schwenk, Muncy, PA
Cathy Sewald, Ft. Collins, CO
Jean Sewald, Longmont, CO
Susan Sewald, Denver, CO
Beverly Shearer, Littleton, CO
Roberta Shrauner, Elkhart, KS
Mary Shupe, Rogers, AR
John Sipe, New Calisto, OH
Katie Smith, Bethel Island, CA
Marline Sommer, Littleton, CO
Dick & Linda Sparks, Midland, TX
Effie Spiking, King City, MO
Sheila Steinberg, Kiowa, CO
Deborah Stewart,
    Pacific Grove, CA
Cindy Stroh, Kiowa, CO
Germaine Tate, Greeley, CO
Patricia Tippett, Aurora, CO
Patsy Tompkins, Peyton, CO
Fanny Warren, Midland, TX
Barbara Webster, Lewellen, NE
Eileen Welch, Midland, TX
Vicki Welch, Adams, CO
Vicky Welch, Midland, TX
Diana West, Oklahoma City, OK
Leona White, Franktown, CO
Maryann Wolff, San Jose, CA
Charlene Womble, Dalhart, TX
Leslie Young, Arvada, CO
Carol Zimmerman, Louisville, CO

A special thank you to our artist, Pam Hake. Pam is a 13 year resident of Elizabeth, Colorado. She received her art degree from the University of Colorado and presently works free lance from her home. She paints in several mediums; watercolor and pastels being her favorites. Pam exhibits at various juried shows throughout Colorado.

IN APPRECIATION

The following people were vital to the creation of this cookbook. They generously shared their favorite recipes with us, making this a delicious sampling of outstanding specialties. We sincerely thank them for their responses, their patience, and their support of our endeavor.

A special thank you to our artist, Pam Hake. Pam is a 17-year resident of Kalispell, Colorado. She received her art degree from the University of Colorado, and presently works full-time from her home. She paints in several mediums: watercolor oil, pastels, and her favorite, Pam exhibits at various juried shows throughout Colorado.

TABLE OF CONTENTS

TABLE OF CONTENTS

APPETIZERS
AND
BEVERAGES

APPETIZERS & BEVERAGES

EASY CHIP DIP

16 oz. cottage cheese
16 oz. sour cream
½ pkg. dry ranch salad
  dressing mixture
Chips

Combine cottage cheese, sour cream and salad dressing mix. Chill for several hours, then serve with chips for dipping.

FRESH SALSA

1 — 16 oz. can tomato bits
  (drain off most of juice)
3 large green onions,
  chopped
1 — 4 oz. can mild green
  chilies, diced
1 tsp. ground cumin
1 tsp. fresh lime juice
1 tsp. sugar
1 tsp. fresh cilantro
½ tsp. pepper
¼ tsp. salt
⅛ tsp. garlic powder

Mix ingredients together in a blender or food processor until consistency is thick but still chunky.

This salsa is a nice change from bottled varieties. The trick is the fresh lime juice and fresh cilantro…try it next time you serve fajitas.

ZIPPY VEGETABLE DIP

1 pint sour cream
1 Tbsp. horseradish
1 Tbsp. minced chives
¼ tsp. garlic powder
1 Tbsp. chopped parsley
1 Tbsp. chopped pimento
  (can use green or red
  bell pepper)
Salt and pepper to taste
Vegetables for dipping

Combine sour cream, horseradish, spices and peppers together. Allow to chill several hours or overnight.

APPETIZERS & BEVERAGES

SWISS CHEESE DIP

1½ cups Swiss cheese,
   shredded
⅓ cup chopped green
   onions
½ cup chopped tomatoes
½ cup mayonnaise

Mix together and serve on party rye bread. This dip is even better if you mix it one day and serve it the next. It is really delicious!

ORANGE FRUIT DIP

1 — 6 oz. frozen orange
   juice concentrate
1½ cups milk
1 — 3.5 oz. pkg. instant
   vanilla pudding
¼ cup sour cream
Fresh fruit: strawberries,
   bananas, apples,
   oranges, grapes,
   cantaloupe, etc.

MAKES 2 CUPS
Put orange juice, milk, and pudding into a blender or food processor. Blend 2 minutes. Stir in sour cream until well mixed.

Makes a great dressing for a fruit salad.

FRESH FRUIT FONDUE

1 — 8 oz. pkg. cream
   cheese, softened
1 — 7 oz. jar marshmallow
   creme
2 Tbsp. grated orange rind
¼ cup orange juice
¼ tsp. ground ginger
Fresh fruit or Angel food
   cake cubes

MAKES 1½ CUPS
Combine cream cheese, marshmallow creme, orange rind, orange juice, and ground ginger and beat until smooth. Dip fresh fruit wedges or angel food cake cubes in mixture.

Try this at your next summertime brunch...it is pretty and delicious, too!

FLAVORFUL FRUIT DIP

12 oz. cream cheese, softened
½ cup sour cream
½ lb. powdered sugar
1 oz. brandy (optional)
½ tsp. lemon extract
½ tsp. vanilla
¼ tsp. almond extract

MAKES 1½ CUPS
Put all ingredients in a food processor and blend until smooth. Serve as a dip with fresh fruit or as a salad dressing.

PINA COLADA DIP

2 — 8 oz. cartons pina colada lowfat yogurt
2 tsp. poppy seed
1 tsp. grated orange peel

MAKES ABOUT 2 CUPS
In a medium bowl, combine all ingredients; blend well. Cover; refrigerate until ready to serve. Serve with fresh fruit dippers. Store in refrigerator.

APPLE DIP

8 oz. light cream cheese
½ cup brown sugar
¾ cup white sugar
1 tsp. vanilla
Sliced apples

Beat cream cheese, sugars, and vanilla until smooth. Chill and serve with sliced apples.

Children love this! Makes a great after-school snack.

Makes a lot
cut recipe in 1/2

6/2019

CRISPY CHEESE SNACKS

½ 1 cup butter, softened
〕 2 cups grated sharp
    Cheddar cheese
½ 1 tsp. salt
〕 2 cups flour
〕 2 cups Rice Krispies
    Cayenne pepper

MAKES 6 DOZEN

In a bowl, thoroughly combine butter, cheese, and salt. Add flour mixing well. Stir in rice cereal. Form dough in ¾-inch balls and flatten with fork or the bottom of a glass on an ungreased baking sheet. Sprinkle lightly with cayenne. Bake at 375° for 10-12 minutes.

These are great appetizers as well as after-school snacks for the kids.

CHUTNEY CHEESE BALL

2 — 8 oz. pkgs. cream
    cheese, softened
½ cup chutney
2 tsp. curry powder
½ tsp. dry mustard
1 cup dried parsley flakes
½ cup chopped pecans

MAKES 1 CHEESE BALL

Combine cream cheese, chutney, curry powder and dry mustard in a bowl or food processor. Blend thoroughly. Sprinkle parsley and nuts on a piece of plastic wrap. Roll cheese into ball and coat with parsley and nuts. Wrap and refrigerate until ready to serve. Serve with crackers.

May be made ahead and frozen.

FRUIT 'N CHEESE BITES

1 cup cottage cheese
1 Tbsp. honey
48 sesame crackers
2 — 11 oz. cans Mandarin
    oranges, drained
2 kiwis, peeled, sliced, and
    halved
Mint sprigs

MAKES 48 APPETIZERS

In a small bowl, mix cottage cheese and honey. Place 1 teaspoonful cottage cheese mixture on each cracker. Top with a kiwi slice, Mandarin orange, and mint sprig.

APPETIZERS & BEVERAGES

MINI CHILI TARTS

1 pkg. refrigerated flaky
 dinner rolls (10)
½ lb. ground beef
¼ tsp. garlic powder
1 — 8 oz. can stewed
 tomatoes
2 Tbsp. tomato paste
3 Tbsp. water
1½ tsp. chili powder
½ tsp. ground red pepper
1 cup shredded Cheddar
 cheese
Salt and pepper to taste

GARNISH:
Sour cream
Guacamole

MAKES ABOUT 40
Separate each dinner roll into 4 layers. Place each section in a greased mini muffin cup, pressing dough onto bottom and sides.

In a large skillet, brown ground beef. Drain. Add garlic powder, tomatoes, tomato paste, water, chili powder, ground red pepper and salt and pepper. Bring to boil. Reduce heat; simmer, uncovered for 20 minutes. Stir occasionally until mixture is thick. Stir in cheese.

Spoon a teaspoon of chili mixture into each muffin cup. Bake at 375° for 15-20 minutes. Remove from pans and serve warm with sour cream or guacamole if desired.

SHERIDA'S CHILI CON QUESO

1 large onion, chopped
2 bell peppers, chopped
1 tsp. garlic powder
2 Tbsp. oil
2 — 7 oz. cans diced green
 chilies
Jalapenos to taste
2 — 2 lb. cans whole
 tomatoes
1 — 2 lb. box Kraft
 American cheese, cut up
Tortilla chips

MAKES LOTS
Saute vegetables in oil with garlic powder for about 3 minutes. Add green chilies, tomatoes, and jalapenos. Simmer on low for 30-45 minutes. Remove from heat and cool. Add the cheese all at once, and stir over low heat to melt. If mixture is too hot, the cheese will curdle. If this happens, add 1 teaspoon baking soda and stir.

Serve with tortilla chips as an appetizer, or pour over chips for nachos.

14

TORTILLA PINWHEELS

FILLING:
1 — 8 oz. carton sour cream
1 — 8 oz. pkg. cream cheese, softened
1 — 4 oz. can green chilies, drained
1 cup grated Cheddar cheese
½ cup chopped green onion
Garlic powder to taste
Seasoned salt to taste

5 — 10-inch flour tortillas
Fresh parsley
Salsa

MAKES 50

Mix filling ingredients together thoroughly. Divide the filling and spread evenly over the tortillas; roll up tortillas. Cover tightly with plastic wrap, twisting ends. Refrigerate for several hours. Unwrap; cut in slices ½-inch to ¾-inch thick. An electric knife works best for this. Lay pinwheels on serving dish. Garnish with parsley. Leave center for small bowl of salsa for dipping.

These are great!

CHEESY CRESCENT NACHOS

1 — 8 oz. can crescent dinner rolls
3 Tbsp. cornmeal
1 — 4 oz. can chopped green chilies, drained
1 cup shredded sharp Cheddar cheese
1 cup shredded Monterey Jack or Mozzarella cheese
Salsa

MAKES 24

Separate dough into 4 rectangles. Coat both sides of each rectangle with cornmeal. Place in ungreased 9 x 13 inch pan; press over bottom and ½ inch up sides to form crust. Seal perforations. Sprinkle with any remaining cornmeal. Sprinkle chilies over crust. Sprinkle cheese over chilies.

Bake at 350° for 22-28 minutes or until crust is golden brown. Cool 5 minutes, then cut into triangles or squares. Serve warm with salsa.

FRUITY CHICKEN SPREAD

2 cups finely chopped
  cooked chicken
1 cup chopped dates
1 cup chopped celery
1 cup pineapple chunks
⅔ cup mayonnaise
¾ cup slivered toasted
  almonds

SERVES 10
Combine chicken, dates, celery, and pineapple. Toss gently with mayonnaise. Refrigerate 1-2 hours. Top with almonds just before serving. Serve with crackers for an unusual and delicious hor d'oeuvre.

For something different, serve as a sandwich spread or on a piece of leaf lettuce.

HORSERADISH SPREAD

1 — 18 oz. jar pineapple
  preserves
1 — 18 oz. jar apple jelly
1 —5 oz. jar prepared
  horseradish, drained
  (use any amount from 1
  Tbsp. to entire jar,
  according to preference)
1 — 1.2 oz. can dry
  mustard
1 Tbsp. cracked black
  pepper
3 — 8 oz. pkg. cream
  cheese
Crackers

MAKES 3½ CUPS
Combine all ingredients, except cream cheese, in a bowl and mix well. To serve, place cream cheese on a serving plate and spoon sauce generously over. Serve with crackers.

This will keep for weeks in a covered jar in the refrigerator...great to have on hand for unexpected company.

APPETIZERS & BEVERAGES

CHEESY POTATO SKINS

3 medium baking potatoes
Vegetable oil
Seasoned salt
1 cup shredded Cheddar
cheese
6 slices bacon, cooked and
crumbled
Sour cream
Chopped green onion

MAKES 1 DOZEN

Scrub potatoes thoroughly, and rub skins with oil; bake at 400° for 1 hour or until done. Cool.

Cut into half lengthwise and scoop out pulp, leaving some potato on the skin. Cut shells in half crosswise and deep fry in hot oil for 2 minutes or until lightly browned. Drain on paper towels. Place skins on a baking sheet and sprinkle with salt, cheese and bacon. Broil until cheese melts. Garnish with a dollop of sour cream and a sprinkling of green onion.

EASY NACHOS

1 — 11 oz. pkg. round
tortilla chips
1 — 16 oz. can refried
beans
½ cup chopped green
onions
1 cup shredded Cheddar
cheese
1 — 12 oz. jar pickled
jalapeno pepper slices

MAKES 3 DOZEN

Place about 3 dozen chips on an ungreased baking sheet. Spread about 2 teaspoons refried beans on each chip; sprinkle with green onions and cheese. Top each with a slice of jalapeno pepper. Bake at 350° for 5 minutes or until cheese melts. (You won't use all the chips or peppers; just save them for the next batch.)

An all-time favorite!

APPENTIZERS & BEVERAGES

MINI QUICHES

1 — 8 oz. can refrigerated
  butterflake dinner rolls
1 —2½ oz. can tiny shrimp,
  drained
1 egg, slightly beaten
½ cup half and half
½ tsp. salt
Dash pepper
1 tsp. chopped pimento
½ tsp. parsley flakes
½ cup shredded Cheddar
  or Gruyere cheese

MAKES 2 DOZEN
Generously grease 24 miniature muffin cups. Separate dough into 12 pieces; divide each roll in half; press dough into muffin cups, covering bottom and sides. Divide shrimp evenly among shells. In small bowl combine egg, half and half, salt, pepper, pimento, and parsley. Spoon about 1 tablespoon mixture into each shell. Sprinkle with cheese. Bake at 375° for 20 minutes or until puffy and lightly browned. Cool slightly. Serve warm.

BRIDGE CLUB SAMPLERS

1 — 8 oz. pkg. cream
  cheese
3 tsp. grated onion
1 cup mayonnaise
½ tsp. cayenne pepper
½ cup Parmesan cheese
4 Tbsp. chives
Bread — white, wheat, rye,
  or your favorite
Garnish: cocktail shrimp,
  diced ham, sprig of
  parsley, etc.

MAKES 6 DOZEN
Mix first six ingredients well. Cut bread with a round cookie cutter, about the size of a half dollar. You can get about 4 rounds to a slice of bread. (You can also use party rye bread.) Spread cheese mixture on each round and quick freeze on a cookie sheet. Store in a freezer bag. Remove as needed, and cook on an ungreased cookie sheet at 350° for 10-15 minutes or until cheese topping is bubbly. Garnish as desired.

18

APPETIZERS & BEVERAGES

COCKTAIL MEATBALLS

1½ lbs. lean ground beef
¾ cup evaporated milk
½ cup chopped onion
1 cup quick oats
1 egg
¼ tsp. garlic powder
¼ tsp. pepper
1 tsp. salt
1 Tbsp. chili powder

SAUCE:
1 cup ketchup
¾ cup brown sugar
¼ tsp. garlic powder
¼ cup chopped onion
1 Tbsp. liquid smoke

MAKES 4 DOZEN
Combine meatball ingredients, shape into balls, and place in one layer in a baking pan.

Combine sauce ingredients and mix well. Pour evenly over meatballs. Bake at 350° for 1 hour. Serve hot.

This dish serves well from a crock pot taken to potluck dinners.

LAURIE'S QUESADILLAS

1 dozen flour tortillas
4-5 cups Cheddar cheese, grated
Butter

OPTIONS:
Diced cooked chicken
Browned hamburger
Salsa
Chopped green onions
Chopped ripe olives

MAKES 36 WEDGES
Butter one side of a flour tortilla, lay in a hot skillet, buttered side down, and sprinkle with cheese. Top with a second tortilla which has been buttered on the top side. Lightly brown tortilla, flip over and brown other side, making sure cheese has melted. Cut into six wedges (like a pie) and serve warm. Can be dipped in sour cream or guacamole.

Vary the plain quesadilla with one or more of the options. You'll find this little treat to be delicious any way you go!

Excellent

1/11

VEGETABLE PIZZA SNACKS

2 — 8 oz. pkgs. crescent
   rolls
2 — 8 oz. pkgs. cream
   cheese
1 tsp. dill weed
⅔ cup mayonnaise
¼ tsp. onion salt
¼ tsp. garlic powder
Chopped veggies:
   broccoli, cauliflower,
   carrots, celery, ripe
   olives, stuffed olives,
   sliced cherry tomatoes,
   green or red pepper,
   black olives, sliced
   mushrooms (Use any of
   these)
Parmesan cheese

MAKES 20 APPETIZERS

Press crescent rolls on greased cookie sheet. Push together to cover, sealing perforations. Bake at 400° for 8-10 minutes.

Combine cream cheese, dill weed, mayonnaise, onion salt, and garlic powder. Spread on cooled crust. Top with your choice of veggies. Sprinkle with Parmesan.

Refrigerate for several hours or overnight. Cut into small pieces.

ELEGANT BAKED CRAB

¾ cup finely diced green
   onion
½ cup finely diced celery
½ cup butter
⅓ cup flour
½ tsp. garlic salt
1½ pints half and half
1 cup processed cheese,
   diced
1 lb. fresh or frozen
   crabmeat
½ cup Parmesan, grated
½ tsp. paprika
Crackers

SERVES 6-10

Saute onions and celery in butter. Add flour, garlic, salt, cream, and cheese. Stir until cheese is melted, add crabmeat and blend. Pour into greased 9 x 9 inch baking dish. Sprinkle Parmesan and paprika over top of mixture and bake at 350° for 20-30 minutes or until lightly browned and bubbly. Serve with crisp cracker rounds.

Your guests will ask for more!

MOLDED SHRIMP SPREAD

1 — 10-oz. can cream of
    shrimp soup, undiluted
6 oz. cream cheese
1 envelope unflavored
    gelatin
2 Tbsp. milk
1 cup chopped celery
1 cup mayonnaise
1 — 4½ oz. can shrimp,
    drained and chopped
    (can use fresh or frozen)
4 green onions, chopped
1 Tbsp. lemon juice
¼ tsp. curry powder

Heat shrimp soup and cheese over low heat until cheese is melted. Stir gelatin into milk until softened. Add to cheese mixture. Stir in remaining ingredients. Pour into 1½ quart mold, and chill several hours until firm. Serve with crackers.

Easy and different!

SHRIMP BITS

20 slices white bread
2 Tbsp. butter or
    margarine, melted
½ tsp. dried whole thyme
¼ lb. frozen, cooked
    shrimp, thawed and
    minced
½ cup shredded Swiss
    cheese
⅓ cup mayonnaise
¼ tsp. salt
Radish slices
Small sprigs of fresh
    dillweed

MAKES ABOUT 3½ DOZEN
Cut each slice of bread into 2 decorative shapes using 2-inch cookie cutters. Make bread crumbs from leftover bread pieces; set aside ½ cup.

Combine butter and thyme; brush over bread cutouts. Place cutouts on cookie sheets; broil 6 inches away from heat for 1 minute or until lightly browned. Cool.

Combine ½ cup reserved bread crumbs, shrimp, cheese, mayonnaise, and salt; mix well and spread on bread cutouts. Bake at 425° for 7 minutes or until bubbly; garnish each with a radish slice and a sprig of dillweed.

APPETIZERS & BEVERAGES

CRAB MOLD

1 — 10 oz. can tomato
   soup
1 — 8 oz. pkg. cream
   cheese
1 envelope unflavored
   gelatin
¼ cup cold water
1 — 6½ oz. can crabmeat
1 cup mayonnaise
¾ cup celery, chopped
¾ cup onion, chopped
1 tsp. Worcestershire
   sauce
¼ tsp. seasoned salt
Crackers
Party rye bread

Heat soup; add cream cheese and mix with a wire whisk. Soften gelatin in ¼ cup cold water, then add to soup mixture. Add rest of ingredients. Spray a mold with Pam or grease lightly with salad oil. Pour mixture into mold and refrigerate overnight. Unmold and serve with crackers or party rye bread.

PECAN-STUFFED MUSHROOMS

16-18 large fresh
   mushrooms
¼ cup butter or margarine,
   divided
2 Tbsp. vegetable oil
2 Tbsp. minced onion
5 slices bacon, cooked and
   crumbled
1 cup soft bread crumbs
4 Tbsp. minced pecans
2 Tbsp. dry sherry
2 Tbsp. sour cream
2 tsp. minced chives
Fresh parsley sprigs
   (optional)

MAKES 1½ DOZEN
Clean mushrooms, removing stems. (Save for a salad or something else.) Heat 2 tablespoons butter and oil in a large skillet. Add mushroom caps; saute 3 minutes on each side. Remove caps with a slotted spoon; place on a baking sheet. Reserve drippings.

Melt 2 tablespoons butter in the skillet with reserved drippings; add onion, and saute until tender. Stir in next 6 ingredients; spoon mixture into mushroom caps. Broil 5 inches from heat for 2-3 minutes. Garnish with parsley, if desired.

IRRESISTIBLE STUFFED MUSHROOMS

2 lbs. large fresh
  mushrooms
1 cup finely chopped onion
3 Tbsp. butter or margarine
1¼ lb. fresh crab, drained
  and flaked
Juice of 1 lemon
⅛ cup chopped fresh
  parsley
1 Tbsp. capers
¾ tsp. Worcestershire
  sauce
Salt to taste
Pepper to taste
⅓ cup mayonnaise
¼ cup dry sherry
Grated Parmesan cheese
⅓ cup butter, melted

MAKES 2 DOZEN

Clean mushrooms with damp paper towels. Remove stems and chop, set aside. Place mushroom caps in a shallow baking pan.

Saute mushroom stems and onion in 3 tablespoons butter in a skillet until tender. Remove from heat and set aside.

Sprinkle crab with lemon juice. Add sauteed mushrooms and next 5 ingredients; mix well. Stir in mayonnaise and sherry. Spoon mushroom mixture into caps; sprinkle with cheese. Drizzle remaining butter over mushrooms. Bake at 350° for 20 minutes.

Extraordinary!

MUSHROOM LOGS

2 — 8 oz. cans refrigerated crescent dinner rolls
1 lb. fresh mushrooms, chopped
4 Tbsp. butter
1 — 8 oz. pkg. cream cheese, softened
1 tsp. seasoned salt
1 egg, beaten
1 to 2 Tbsp. poppy seeds

MAKES 4 DOZEN

Separate crescent dough into 8 rectangles; press perforations to seal.

Saute mushrooms in butter until cooked. Drain. Combine with cream cheese and salt. Spread in equal portions over each rectangle of dough. Starting at long sides, roll up each rectangle jellyroll fashion; pinch seams to seal. Slice logs into 1-inch pieces; place seam side down on an ungreased baking sheet.

Brush each log with beaten eggs, and sprinkle with poppy seeds. Bake at 375° for 10-12 minutes.

PARTY CRUNCHERS

8 cups Crispix cereal
2½ cups bite-size Cheddar cheese crackers
2½ cups pretzels
¼ cup vegetable oil
1 packet (1 oz.) dry ranch salad dressing mix

MAKES 13 CUPS

Combine cereal, crackers, pretzels, and oil. Spread on a 9 x 13 inch pan and bake at 250° for 15 minutes, stirring after 10 minutes. (Mixture can be microwaved on high for 1 minute in a large microwave-safe bowl.)

Place dressing mix in a 2 gallon zip-lock bag. Add cereal mixture, seal bag, and shake until cereal is thoroughly coated. Store in an airtight container.

PARTY MIX

7 cups Crispix cereal
1 cup salted mixed nuts
1 cup pretzels
3 Tbsp. margarine, melted
¼ tsp. garlic salt
¼ tsp. onion salt
2 tsp. lemon juice
4 tsp. Worcestershire
   sauce

MAKES 9 CUPS
Combine cereal, nuts, and pretzels in a large bowl. Stir together remaining ingredients in a smaller bowl, then toss gently with cereal. Spread in a 9 x 13 inch pan and bake at 250° for 45 minutes, stirring every 15 minutes. Spread on paper towels to cool. Store in an airtight container. (Can also be microwaved on high 4 minutes, stirring after 2 minutes.)

This mix is a wonderful Christmas gift when given in a holiday tin.

CAPPUCCINO

½ gallon vanilla ice cream
½ gallon chocolate ice
   cream
1 pint half and half
1½ cups strong coffee
2 jiggers each Kahlua,
   brandy, and rum

SERVES 8
Melt ice cream on low heat in large pan and add rest of ingredients. Blend well. Serve hot.

This delicious dessert drink is the perfect way to end your next dinner party!

INSTANT HOT CHOCOLATE MIX

1 — 2 lb. box Nestles
   chocolate mix
1 lb. powdered sugar
1 — 11 oz. jar powdered
   non-dairy creamer
1 — 8 quart box powdered
   milk

MAKES 50 SERVINGS
Mix all ingredients and sift together. Store in airtight jar. To serve, fill a mug half full of mix and finish filling with hot water.

Great to have on hand...easy for kids to heat up themselves.

APPETIZERS & BEVERAGES

PERCOLATOR PUNCH

3 cups unsweetened
   pineapple juice
3 cups cranberry juice
1½ cups cold water
⅓ cup brown sugar,
   packed
2 lemon slices
2 (4 inch) cinnamon sticks,
   broken
1½ tsp. whole cloves

MAKES 7 CUPS
Pour juices and water into a 12-cup percolator. Place remaining ingredients, except cinnamon sticks, in percolator basket. Perk through complete cycle. Serve with cinnamon stick, if desired.

This is a great punch to serve for a Christmas caroling party...the aroma is wonderful, not to mention the flavor!

MOCHA PUNCH

1 quart strong cold coffee
1 quart chocolate ice
   cream
1 quart vanilla ice cream
1 cup whipping cream
¼ tsp. salt
½ cup sugar
¼ tsp. almond extract
½ tsp. vanilla
½ tsp. nutmeg
¼ tsp. cinnamon

SERVES 35
Pour cold coffee into a punch bowl. Add small chunks of ice cream. Whip cream, adding salt, sugar, almond extract and vanilla; fold into punch. Sprinkle with nutmeg and cinnamon.

SPICED ICED TEA

3 cups boiling water
5 regular-size cinnamon/
apple flavored tea bags
1½ cups sugar
1 — 6 oz. can frozen
lemonade concentrate,
thawed
1 — 6 oz. can frozen
orange juice
concentrate, thawed
2 cups unsweetened
pineapple juice
9 cups water
Lemon slices

MAKES 1 GALLON
Pour boiling water over tea bags; cover and steep 5 minutes. Remove tea bags, squeezing gently. Stir in sugar, juice concentrates, pineapple juice and 9 cups water. Chill. Serve over ice. Garnish each serving with lemon slices if desired.

SUMMER SLUSH

1 — 6 oz. can frozen
lemonade concentrate
1 — 6 oz. can frozen
orange juice concentrate
1 juice can water
1 juice can rum

SERVES 6-8
Combine all ingredients in a 1-quart freezer container, such as a plastic bowl with a lid. Freeze overnight. Spoon into champagne glasses to serve.

CREAMY STRAWBERRY DAIQUIRIS

1 cup crushed ice
1 cup sliced fresh
strawberries
½ cup light rum
⅓ cup frozen pink
lemonade concentrate,
thawed
1 pint vanilla ice cream

MAKES 1 QUART
Combine all ingredients in blender or food processor. Blend until smooth. Serve immediately.

APPETIZERS & BEVERAGES

4-H CLUB PUNCH

4 envelopes unsweetened
  cherry Kool-Aid drink
  mix
4 cups sugar
8 quarts water
4 — 46 oz. cans tropical
  fruit punch
4 — 46 oz. cans pineapple
  juice
4 — 33 oz. bottles ginger
  ale, chilled

MAKES 5-6 GALLONS
Blend Kool-Aid, sugar, and water.
Add fruit punch and pineapple juice.
Chill; add ginger ale just before serv-
ing. Other flavors of the Kool-Aid
may be substituted.

CRANBERRY SPRITZER

1½ cups cranberry juice
1½ cups orange juice
1½ cups 7-Up
Maraschino cherries

SERVES 4
Combine juices to blend. Slowly
pour in 7-Up. Serve over ice. Garnish with a maraschino cherry, if
desired.
Great party drink for kids.

PEACH COOLER

1 quart peach ice cream
  (use a good brand)
½ to ¾ cup amaretto
2-4 Tbsp. white rum

SERVES 4
Place all ingredients in blender or
food processor. Blend just until ingredients are mixed. Pour into
stemmed glasses and serve. Makes
a great summer brunch drink.

PINEAPPLE SNOWSTORM

1 pint vanilla ice cream,
  softened
1½ cups pineapple juice
1 cup club soda

SERVES 4
In a blender or food processor, beat
softened ice cream. Gradually add
pineapple juice, then club soda to
blend. Serve immediately.

BRUNCH

BRUNCH

SPICY POTATO QUICHE

1 — 24 oz. pkg. frozen
   shredded hashed
   browns, thawed
⅓ cup melted butter
1 cup shredded hot pepper
   cheese
1 cup shredded Swiss
   cheese
1 cup diced cooked ham
½ cup half and half
2 eggs
¼ tsp. seasoned salt

SERVES 6

Remove moisture from thawed hash browns by pressing between paper towels. Fit hash browns into a greased 10-inch pie plate, forming a solid crust. Brush with melted butter. Bake at 425° for 25 minutes. Remove from oven and sprinkle cheeses and ham evenly over crust. Beat half and half with eggs and salt. Pour over cheese and ham. Bake uncovered at 350° for 30-40 minutes or until knife inserted in middle comes out clean.

CHILIQUILLES

10-12 corn tortillas, cut into
   strips ½-inch wide and
   2-inches long
1 onion, chopped
4 Tbsp. butter
1 dozen eggs, beaten
¼ cup milk
¼ tsp. garlic juice
Salt and pepper to taste
1 — 4 oz. can green chilies
½ cup grated Cheddar
   cheese
1 tomato, peeled and
   chopped

SERVES 8

Saute tortilla strips and onion in butter until softened. Beat eggs, add milk, garlic juice, salt and pepper. Pour over tortilla mixture. Cook, stirring until soft scrambled. Add green chilies, cheese and tomato. Stir until cheese melts.

Try this for midnight breakfast after a night on the town!

BRUNCH CASSEROLE

1 lb. bulk pork sausage
1 — 8 oz. can crescent
   dinner rolls
2 cups shredded
   Mozzarella cheese
4 eggs, beaten
¾ cup milk
¼ tsp. salt
⅛ tsp. pepper

SERVES 6

Crumble sausage in skillet and brown over medium heat until cooked. Drain. Line bottom of greased 9 x 13 inch baking dish with rolls, firmly pressing perforations in rolls to seal. Sprinkle rolls with sausage and cheese. Combine remaining ingredients. Beat well and pour over sausage. Bake at 425° for 15-20 minutes or until set. Let stand 5 minutes. Cut into squares and serve immediately.

FRENCH TOAST SUPPER

8 thick slices (¾-inch)
   French or sourdough
   bread
4 slices Canadian bacon
4 slices Monterey Jack
   cheese
½ cup eggnog
Powdered sugar, optional
Strawberry preserves,
   optional

SERVES 4

Stack 1 slice Canadian bacon and 1 slice cheese between every 2 pieces of French bread. (Cut or overlap bacon and cheese to fit on bread.) Dip sandwich in eggnog, thoroughly covering both sides. Brown over medium heat in a lightly greased skillet (use nonstick spray) until sandwiches are hot, cheese is melted, and both sides are nicely browned. Sift powdered sugar over each sandwich and serve with strawberry preserves.

BRUNCH

FRIED GRITS

4 cups water
½ tsp. salt
1 cup uncooked quick-
  cooking grits
2 Tbsp. cooked, crumbled
  bacon
5 Tbsp. butter, divided

SERVES 8

Bring water and salt to a boil; stir in grits. Cook grits until done, following package directions. Remove from heat. Add bacon and 1 tablespoon butter; stir until butter melts.

Pour grits into a greased loaf pan. Cool; cover and refrigerate over-night. Remove grits by inverting pan; cut loaf into ½ inch slices. Melt remaining ¼ cup butter in large skillet; fry slices over medium heat 5-7 minutes or until lightly browned, turning once.

Good old Southern grits can't be beat!

TEXAS EGGS

2 dozen eggs
½ cup milk
½ stick margarine
8 strips bacon, fried and
  crumbled
½ onion, chopped
½ green pepper, chopped
2 — 4 oz. cans mushrooms
2 — 10 oz. cans cream of
  mushroom soup
½ cup white wine
2 cups grated Cheddar
  cheese

SERVES 10-12

Beat eggs together with milk. Scramble until cooked in hot margarine. Spread in a 9 x 13 inch pan. Top with bacon, onion, green pepper, and mushrooms. Warm soup together with wine and spread over mixture. Top with cheese. Cover with foil and refrigerate overnight. Uncover and bake 50 minutes at 300°.

OPEN-FACE EGG SANDWICHES

1½ Tbsp. butter or
  margarine
1½ Tbsp. flour
¾ milk
¾ cup shredded Cheddar
  cheese
Salt and pepper
4 eggs
2 Tbsp. water
2 Tbsp. butter or
  margarine, divided
4 tomato slices, cut ¼ inch
  thick
4 slices buttered toast
Chopped fresh parsley,
  optional

SERVES 4

Melt butter in a heavy saucepan over low heat; add flour, stirring until smooth. Cook 1 minute, stirring constantly. Gradually add milk, stirring until thickened and bubbly. Add cheese, dash of salt and pepper, stirring until smooth. Set aside.

Combine eggs, water and a dash of salt and pepper; beat well. Melt 1 tablespoon butter in a 10 inch skillet. Add egg mixture, and cook over low heat until eggs are partially set; stir occasionally until the eggs are firm but still moist.

Fry tomato slices in remaining 1 tablespoon butter, 1 minute on each side. Place a tomato slice on each piece of toast. Spoon eggs over tomato, and top with cheese sauce. Garnish with parsley if desired.

This is an easy dish to make and one that is guaranteed to please everyone in your family!

BRUNCH

GOOD MORNING!

2 lbs. bulk sausage
2 medium potatoes,
   chopped
1 medium onion, chopped
1 green pepper, chopped
Garlic salt, to taste
Black pepper, to taste
Jalapeno pepper, chopped
   to taste
5-6 eggs, beaten
1 lb. Velveeta cheese, cut
   into chunks

SERVES 4-6
Cook first seven ingredients slowly in a large skillet. Drain as mixture cooks. Add eggs and cheese. Cook until eggs are done. Can add salsa or picante sauce to taste. Serve plain or with tortillas.

FANCY FRENCH TOAST

1 — 1 lb. loaf unsliced
   white bread
4 eggs
1 cup milk
2 Tbsp. Grand Marnier
   liqueur
1 Tbsp. sugar
½ tsp. vanilla
¼ tsp. salt
¼ tsp. freshly grated
   orange peel
Vegetable oil
3 Tbsp. butter, melted
Powdered sugar
1 orange, thinly sliced,
   optional

SERVES 4
Slice bread into eight ¾-inch slices. In a medium bowl, beat eggs with milk, Grand Marnier, sugar, vanilla, salt and orange peel until well blended. Dip each piece of bread into liquid mixture until saturated. Place in a flat baking dish. Pour remaining liquid over bread. Cover and refrigerate overnight.

In skillet, heat oil and saute bread until golden on both sides. Brush with butter and sprinkle with powdered sugar. Top with orange slice and serve immediately with maple syrup.

SOUR CREAM PANCAKES

½ tsp. baking soda
1 cup sour cream
1 cup buttermilk
1 tsp. salt
1 tsp. baking powder
2 Tbsp. sugar
2 cups flour
4 eggs
½ tsp. vanilla

SERVES 4

Stir soda in a small amount of sour cream; set aside. Mix remaining sour cream and buttermilk, add baking powder, salt, sugar, and flour. Mix well. Add eggs one at a time, mixing after each addition. Add sour cream with soda and vanilla. Mix well. For thin pancakes add small amount of milk until it is desired consistency.

Pour onto hot griddle or skillet. Serve with warmed syrup and fresh fruit.

SKILLET SUPPER

6 slices bacon
1 medium potato, peeled and diced
1 medium onion, chopped
6 eggs
¾ tsp. salt
⅛ tsp. pepper
½ cup Cheddar cheese, grated

SERVES 4

Fry bacon in a 10-inch skillet until crisp. Remove and crumble. Drain drippings, reserving 4 tablespoons. Add potato and onion to reserved bacon drippings and cook over medium heat until potato is tender. Stir bacon into potato mixture. Beat eggs with salt and pepper. Stir into potato mixture. Top with cheese.

Cover and cook over low heat until eggs are set and light brown on bottom. If bottom is cooking too fast, remove from heat and keep covered until set. Cut into wedges and serve.

Try this on Sunday night or any mealtime when you want a nutritious meal without a big production!

BRUNCH

DAVEY'S SPECIAL

1 lb. mild pork sausage
1 lb. hash browns, loose
1½ cups Cheddar cheese,
    grated
1 — 4 oz. can diced green
    chilies
¼ cup chopped green
    pepper
8 eggs
Salt
Pepper

SERVES 6

Crumble sausage in a hot skillet and brown until cooked through. In same skillet, add hash browns, cover and cook on low until potatoes are done, stirring occasionally. Add the cheese, green chilies and green pepper. Whisk eggs and stir into sausage mixture. Scramble all ingredients together until eggs are done. Salt and pepper to taste.

This recipe is delicious as is, or it can be rolled in a flour tortilla for a breakfast burrito.

CHARLIE'S BREAKFAST BURRITOS

2 lb. bacon, cut up
1 lb. chorizo sausage
1 medium onion, chopped
1 green pepper, chopped
3 dozen eggs
2 — 10 oz. cans Ro-Tel
    tomatoes
Flour tortillas

SERVES 15

Fry bacon in a large skillet. Remove and drain. In the same skillet, brown the chorizo sausage and the chopped vegetables until tender. Remove vegetables, and drain most of the grease, leaving just enough to cover the bottom of the skillet. In a large bowl, whisk the eggs until foamy. Stir in Ro-Tel tomatoes and scramble in the large skillet.

When halfway done, stir in bacon, sausage, and vegetables. Continue to cook until eggs are cooked. Spoon into a warmed flour tortilla. What a way to start the day!

MIGAS

1 pkg. corn tortillas
½ cup oil
½ tsp. garlic powder
1 medium onion, chopped
2 tomatoes, diced
¼ cup butter
2 dozen eggs
10 oz. medium sharp
   Cheddar cheese, grated
10 oz. Monterey Jack
   cheese, grated
Salt and pepper to taste

SERVES 10-12
Fry corn tortillas in oil until crisp. Saute garlic, onion, and tomatoes in butter until tender. Beat eggs with salt and pepper. Add egg mixture to tomato mixture. Cook over medium-low heat until soft. Crumble fried chips and add to eggs along with the cheeses. Stir until cheeses melt and chips are softened.

This is a wonderful variation of scrambled eggs. Serve with warmed tortillas (flour or corn) and butter.

BRUNCH PIE

8 slices bacon, fried crisp
1 Tbsp. reserved bacon
   drippings
½ cup corn flake crumbs
5 eggs
2½ cups frozen hashed
   brown potatoes
1½ cups Swiss cheese,
   grated
⅓ cup milk
1 green onion, thinly sliced
1 tsp. salt
⅛ tsp. pepper
4 drops Tabasco sauce

SERVES 6
Crumble bacon and set aside. Mix corn flakes with reserved bacon drippings and set aside. In a medium-sized bowl, beat eggs until foamy. Stir in remaining ingredients. Pour into greased 9-inch pie pan. Sprinkle with crumb mixture and bacon. Cover and refrigerate overnight. Cover and bake at 325° for 50 minutes or until knife inserted in center comes out clean.

BRUNCH

FARMER'S BREAKFAST

¼ cup chopped onion
¼ cup butter or margarine
2 medium potatoes, peeled
  and chopped
1 tsp. water
¼ tsp. salt
6 eggs
¼ tsp. salt
Dash pepper
2 Tbsp. milk
1 cup diced ham
2 Tbsp. Cheddar cheese,
  grated

SERVES 4

In a skillet, cook onion in butter or margarine until tender. Add potatoes, water and salt. Cover and cook over medium heat, about 10 minutes, or until potatoes are done.

Beat together eggs, milk, salt and pepper; stir in ham. Pour this mixture over potatoes. Stir and cook over medium heat until egg mixture is about half done. Add cheese, and continue to cook until eggs are done. Serve immediately. Top each serving with a tablespoon of picante sauce for a little added zing!

MINI MEXICAN QUICHES

1 — 11 oz. pkg. refrigerated
  buttermilk biscuits
1 cup shredded Monterey
  Jack cheese
9 eggs, slightly beaten
⅓ cup milk
½ cup chopped onion
½ cup chopped green
  pepper
⅓ cup chopped pimento
½ tsp. salt
¼ tsp. hot pepper sauce
5 black olives, halved
Cayenne pepper

MAKES 10

On a lightly floured board, roll out each biscuit to a 5½-inch circle. Pat circles into 10 greased muffin or custard cups. Dough should come just to top of cups. Sprinkle 1 tablespoon cheese into each cup; reserve remaining cheese. Mix eggs, milk, onion, green pepper, pimento, salt, and pepper sauce in a medium bowl with a whisk. Pour about ¼ cup egg mixture over cheese in each cup. Bake 25 minutes at 375° or until a wooden pick inserted in center comes out clean. Sprinkle about ½ tablespoon cheese on each egg cup. Top with an olive half. Bake 1 minute more or until cheese melts. Sprinkle with cayenne pepper.

COUNTRY CORNBREAD BRUNCH

3 Tbsp. butter or margarine
3 Tbsp. flour
2 cups milk
¼ tsp. salt
⅛ tsp. pepper
6 hard-cooked eggs,
   chopped
½ cup mayonnaise

CORNBREAD:
1 cup yellow cornmeal
1 cup flour
¼ cup sugar
4 tsp. baking powder
½ tsp. salt
1 cup milk
1 egg
¼ cup vegetable oil

GARNISH:
Chopped green onion
8-10 slices bacon, cooked
   and crumbled
Shredded Cheddar cheese

SERVES 8

Melt butter in a heavy saucepan over low heat; add flour, stirring until smooth. Cook 1 minute, stirring constantly. Gradually add milk; cook until thickened and bubbly, stirring constantly. Add salt and next 3 ingredients; cook, stirring, until thoroughly heated.

To make cornbread, combine ingredients in a bowl and mix until well blended. Pour into a greased 10-inch pie pan and bake at 425° for 20-25 minutes.

To serve, cut cornbread into wedges, and slice in half horizontally. Spoon egg mixture on cornbread wedges, and sprinkle with green onions, bacon, and cheese.

COUNTRY CORNBREAD BRUNCH

3 Tbsp. butter or margarine
1 Tbsp. flour
2 cups milk
¼ tsp. salt
⅛ tsp. pepper
6 hard-cooked eggs, chopped
½ cup mayonnaise

CORNBREAD:
1 cup yellow cornmeal
1 cup flour
¼ cup sugar
4 tsp. baking powder
½ tsp. salt
1 cup milk
1 egg
¼ cup vegetable oil

GARNISH:
Chopped green onion
8-10 slices bacon, cooked and crumbled
Shredded Cheddar cheese

SERVES 6

Melt butter in a heavy saucepan over low heat. Add flour, stirring until smooth. Cook 1 minute, stirring constantly. Gradually add milk; cook until thickened and bubbly, stirring constantly. Add salt and next 3 ingredients; cook, stirring, until thoroughly heated.

To make cornbread, combine ingredients in a bowl and mix until well blended. Pour into a greased 10-inch pie pan and bake at 425° for 20-25 minutes.

To serve, cut cornbread into wedges and slice in half horizontally. Spoon egg mixture over cornbread wedges, and garnish with green onions, bacon, and cheese.

SOUPS AND
SANDWICHES

SOUPS & SANDWICHES

BARLEY SOUP

¾ cup medium pearl barley
11 cups chicken broth
3 Tbsp. butter
1½ cups minced onion
1 cup minced carrot
1 cup thinly sliced
   mushrooms (save a few
   for garnish)
½ cup minced celery
Salt and pepper

GARNISH:
Minced parsley
¼ cup sour cream
Reserved mushroom slices

SERVES 6-8
In a saucepan, combine barley and 3 cups chicken broth. Bring to a boil, reduce heat, and simmer until liquid is absorbed, about 1 hour.

In a large Dutch oven or stew pot, melt butter and saute onion, carrot, mushroom slices and celery for five minutes until softened. Add 8 cups chicken broth and simmer, uncovered 30 minutes. Add cooked barley and simmer 5 minutes. Add salt and pepper to taste.

Garnish with dollop of sour cream, sliced mushrooms and parsley sprinkles.

Delicious as a first course for a holiday dinner party.

BIG AL'S BLACK BEAN SOUP

1 lb. black beans
1 ham bone, with some
   meat left on
1 cup chopped onions
1 cup chopped carrots
1 cup chopped celery
1 tsp. salt
¼ tsp. pepper

SERVES 6
Place beans in a large Dutch oven. Cover with 2 inches of water. Soak 6-8 hours. Add ham bone and bring to a boil. Lower heat and simmer, covered, about 2 hours. Add veggies, salt and pepper and stir to mix. Simmer, covered, for 1 more hour.

SOUPS & SANDWICHES

JESSI'S BEAN SOUP

2 — 15 oz. cans butter
    beans
1 — 10 oz. can Ro-Tel
    tomatoes
1 — 10 oz. can diced
    tomatoes
1 — 12 oz. pkg. hot dogs,
    sliced
2 tsp. dried minced onion
1 tsp. sugar
1 tsp. ground cumin
1 tsp. instant chicken
    bouillon granules
½ tsp. pepper
1 cup shredded Cheddar
    cheese

SERVES 6

In a large saucepan, stir together everything but the Cheddar cheese. Bring to a boil. Reduce heat and simmer, uncovered about 10 minutes or until heated through, stirring occasionally. Ladle into bowls. Sprinkle each serving with cheese.

This is a great soup for kids to make...delicious and good for you, too!

SPLIT PEA SOUP

2 cups dried peas
2 quarts water
1 ham bone
1 cup celery, chopped
½ cup onion, chopped
½ cup carrots, sliced
1 bay leaf
¼ tsp. thyme
Salt and pepper to taste

SERVES 6

Wash peas; add water. Bring to a boil and simmer 2 minutes. Remove from heat; cover and let stand 1 hour. Add ham bone, vegetables, bay leaf and thyme; heat to boiling. Reduce heat and simmer, covered, for 2½ to 3 hours or until peas are soft. Remove bone; cut off meat and dice. If desired, put vegetables in food processor or blender. Return meat and vegetables to soup; season to taste.

GUMBO

¾ cup bacon drippings
¾ cup flour
2 — 10 oz. pkg. frozen
  chopped okra
1 green bell pepper,
  chopped
4 stalks celery, chopped
4 green onions, chopped
½ tsp. garlic powder
8 cups chicken broth
1 — 6 oz. can tomato paste
2 tsp. pepper
1 tsp. paprika
2 tsp. salt
4 beef bouillon cubes
2-3 quarts cooked chicken,
  chunked, and/or raw,
  peeled, deveined shrimp
Tabasco to taste
Cooked rice

MAKES 5-6 QUARTS
In a large stockpot, melt bacon drippings. Add flour and stir constantly over medium to low heat until roux is a dark brown. DO NOT BURN. This process takes about 30 minutes, but is the key to a successful gumbo.

Lower heat and add okra, green pepper, celery, onions, and garlic powder. Saute until onions are soft. Add stock, tomato paste, seasonings, and bouillon cubes. Simmer for 2 hours. Add chicken and/or shrimp. (I like to use both…turkey may be substituted for chicken) 15 minutes before serving. Add Tabasco to taste. Serve over mounds of hot rice in a large soup bowl. This recipe makes a lot and freezes well, so I've found it easier to make this whole recipe, use what I need, and freeze the rest.

Gumbo is a wonderful original creation of South Louisiana. The okra serves as a thickening agent, but file, the powdered sassafras leaf, is the true Cajun method. Choctaw Indians used file and their word for sassafras — Kombo — is the origin of the term "gumbo." If you choose to use file in your gumbo, add it after the soup is removed from the heat, just before serving. Gumbo is subject to a multitude of variations…use bits of ham, turkey, duck, sausage, seafood or bacon to flavor your creation. You will love it!

SOUPS & SANDWICHES

SOUP ITALIANO

1½ lbs. Italian sausage
½ cup chopped onion
1 — 28 oz. can Italian-style
  tomatoes, undrained
  and chopped
4 small potatoes, peeled
  and cubed
1 cup chopped celery,
  leaves and all
¼ cup chopped fresh
  parsley
7 cups water
1 beef-flavored bouillon
  cube
2 Tbsp. sugar
1 Tbsp. lemon juice
½ bay leaf
¼ tsp. dried whole thyme
¼ tsp. pepper

MAKES 2½ QUARTS
Brown sausage in a large Dutch oven; add onion and cook, stirring constantly. Add remaining ingredients. Bring to a boil; cover, reduce heat, and simmer 45 minutes. Remove bay leaf.

This is delicious with herbed French bread and a salad.

CREAMY TURNIP SOUP

4 cups turnips, peeled and
  thinly slice
2 medium onions, sliced
1 large carrot, sliced
1 stalk celery, chopped
1½ tsp. salt
1 tsp. sugar
⅛ tsp. pepper
1 cup water
3 cups milk
1 cup half and half
2 Tbsp. butter

SERVES 4
Combine first 8 ingredients in a stockpot. Bring to a boil; reduce heat and simmer 15-20 minutes or until vegetables are tender. In a blender or food processor, puree until smooth.

Return to stockpot, stir in milk, half and half, and butter. Cook over low heat, stirring constantly until heated through. Serve immediately.

SOPA DE MAIZ

3½ cups corn kernels
(fresh or frozen)
1 cup chicken broth
4 Tbsp. butter
2 cups milk
1 tsp. cumin
¼ tsp. garlic powder
1 — 4 oz. can diced green
chilies
3 dashes Tabasco sauce
1 tsp. ground white pepper
1 cup diced tomatoes
2 cups diced cooked
chicken
1 cup shredded Monterey
Jack cheese with
jalapenos
Corn tortilla chips

CONDIMENTS:
Chunky salsa
Sliced black olives
Sour cream
Sliced green onions
Diced avocados

SERVES 6-8

In a blender or food processor, puree corn and broth. Melt butter in Dutch oven. Add corn puree and simmer over low for 5 minutes, stirring constantly. Stir in milk, cumin and garlic. Heat to boiling, reduce heat and stir in green chilies, Tabasco, and pepper.

Put equal amounts of diced tomatoes and chicken in individual soup bowls. Add shredded cheese to simmering soup and stir until cheese melts. Spoon soup into bowls and garnish with chips. Condiments can be added individually as desired.

This is a great main dish soup.

MEXICAN MEATBALL SOUP

1 beaten egg
¾ cup soft bread crumbs
   (1 slice)
2 Tbsp. finely chopped
   onion
½ tsp. chili powder
¾ lb. ground beef
1 Tbsp. cooking oil
½ cup chopped onion
⅓ cup chopped green
   pepper
1 — 16 oz. can diced
   tomatoes
1 — 8 oz. can tomato sauce
1 —15 oz. can kidney
   beans, drained
2 Tbsp. parsley, chopped
½ cup water
¼ tsp. crushed red pepper
Salt and pepper to taste
Shredded Cheddar cheese

MAKES 4 MAIN DISH SERVINGS
Combine egg, bread crumbs, onion, chili powder and ground beef. Mix well. Shape into 24 1-inch meatballs. Heat oil in a Dutch oven. Brown meatballs, 12 at a time, in oil. Remove and drain. In reserved drippings, cook onion and green pepper until tender. Drain off excess fat. Add meatballs, undrained tomatoes, tomato sauce, beans, parsley, water, and red pepper. Bring to boil; reduce heat. Salt and pepper to taste. Cover and simmer 30 minutes or until vegetables are tender. Sprinkle cheese on top of each serving.

WILD RICE SOUP

3 Tbsp. butter
⅓ cup minced onion
¼ cup flour
4 cups chicken broth
2 cups cooked wild rice
⅔ cup ham, chopped
⅓ cup celery, chopped
2 carrots, finely grated
1 cup half and half
3 Tbsp. almonds, slivered
Minced parsley

SERVES 4-5
Melt butter in saucepan, saute onion until tender. Blend in flour and gradually add chicken broth, stirring until smooth. Cook, stirring constantly until mixture thickens slightly. Stir in rice, ham, celery and carrots. Simmer about 30 minutes. Stir in half and half and almonds. Heat through and serve. Garnish with minced parsley.

This recipe came to us by way of North Dakota...it is really tasty!

SOUPS & SANDWICHES

SOPA DE LA CASA

8 slices bacon, diced
1¼ cups onion, finely
   chopped
1¼ cups celery, finely
   chopped
2 small green peppers,
   finely chopped
2 cloves garlic, minced
2 — 14 oz. cans chicken
   broth
2 — 16 oz. cans refried
   beans
½ tsp. pepper
2 Tbsp. chili powder
Shredded Monterey Jack
   cheese
Tortilla chips

SERVES 8

In a large Dutch oven, cook bacon until crisp. Drain half of bacon drippings. Add onion, celery, and green pepper. Cook until tender; add garlic. Blend in chicken broth, refried beans, pepper and chili powder. Bring to a boil and remove from heat immediately. Garnish with cheese and serve with chips.

This hearty soup will become a standard on cold winter nights…especially easy on the cook and satisfying to the family.

OYSTER STEW

¼ cup butter or margarine
3 leeks, chopped (white
   part only)
2 potatoes, peeled and
   diced
2 carrots, peeled and
   sliced
2 cups water
3 chicken bouillon cubes
2 cups milk
2 cups half and half
¼ tsp. cayenne pepper
4 — 6 oz. cans oysters,
   undrained
Salt and pepper to taste
Fresh chopped parsley

SERVES 4

In a large soup kettle, melt butter and saute leeks until tender (about 10 minutes). Add potatoes, carrot, water and bouillon cubes. Cover and simmer 20 minutes until potatoes are tender. Allow mixture to cool, then puree in blender or food processor. Return puree to kettle and add all remaining ingredients. Heat through but do not boil.

WON-TON SOUP

½ lb. ground pork
¼ cup green onion, chopped fine
1 Tbsp. cooking wine
1 Tbsp. oil
¼ tsp. pepper
2 Tbsp. soy sauce
½ tsp. salt
¼ cup cabbage, chopped very fine
Won-ton wrappings
1 — 10½ oz. can chicken broth
2 soup cans water
Mushrooms (optional)
Chopped celery (optional)

SERVES 6-8

Put pork, onion, wine, oil, pepper, soy sauce, salt and cabbage into a large bowl and mix well. Hold a wrapping in your palm and place a tablespoon of the filling in the center of the wrapping. Fold the corner nearest you to the opposite corner to form a triangle with its base facing you. Wet the two corners with a drop of water and pinch together. Turn the triangle around so that the top is pointing toward you. Hold the other two corners and fold upward. Wet corners and pinch together.

To prepare soup, combine broth and water in a pot. Bring it to a boil. Drop prepared won-ton into it and cook for 5-10 minutes or until soup boils again. Add mushrooms or celery. Boil 2-3 minutes and serve.

SOUPS & SANDWICHES

ITALIAN SAUSAGE SOUP

1 lb. Italian sausage
2 cups sliced celery
2 — 28 oz. cans diced
   tomatoes
1 cup chopped onion
1 tsp. salt
1 tsp. sugar
1 tsp. oregano
1 tsp. Italian seasoning
½ tsp. basil
¼ tsp. garlic powder
6 small zucchini, cut into
   ¼ inch slices
1 medium green pepper,
   chopped
1 cup water
1 cup red wine

MAKES 3 QUARTS
Brown sausage in a Dutch oven until
done. Add celery and cook until tender; drain. Add next 8 ingredients.
Cover, reduce heat, and simmer 20
minutes. Add remaining ingredients;
cover and simmer 20 minutes more
or until vegetables are tender.

CAJUN CHICKEN SANDWICH

4 — 5 oz. boneless,
   skinned chicken breasts
4 Tbsp. butter
Cajun seasoning
4 Kaiser or hamburger
   buns

SERVES 4
In a skillet, saute chicken pieces in
butter. Sprinkle Cajun seasoning liberally over both sides of chicken
pieces. Cook over medium heat until
done throughout. Remove and place
on bun. Add lettuce, cheese, tomato,
mustard or mayonnaise if desired.

Easy and different!

CALZONES

1 loaf frozen bread dough,
  thawed
1 lb. mild Italian sausage
1 cup shredded Provolone
  cheese
1 cup shredded Mozzarella
  cheese
½ cup Ricotta cheese
¼ cup Parmesan cheese
¼ tsp. dried basil
¼ tsp. salt
¼ tsp. pepper
¼ tsp. dried rosemary
1 egg white

SERVES 10-12
Roll out bread dough on floured counter to ¼-½ inch thickness. In medium skillet, cook sausage and drain. Combine sausage, cheeses, basil, salt, pepper and rosemary and mix well. Spread over dough. Roll up carefully so loaf looks like long loaf of French bread. Seal long edge and tuck under ends. Place rolled loaf on greased cookie sheet, seam side down. Glaze with egg white. Bake at 350° for 30-40 minutes or until golden brown. Slice into ¾ inch slices.

CHEESE AND ONION PASTRIES

1 cup shredded Cheddar
  cheese
¼ cup sliced green onions
2 — 8 oz. cans refrigerated
  crescent dinner rolls
2 tsp. butter
¼ tsp. dried dill weed
  OR
Egg white, beaten
Sesame seeds

MAKES 16
In a small bowl, combine cheese and onions. Separate dough into 16 triangles. Place rounded teaspoonful cheese mixture on center of each triangle. Bring corners to center over filling, overlapping ends; press gently to seal. Place on ungreased cookie sheet. Brush each lightly with butter; sprinkle with dill weed. (Or brush with beaten egg white, then sprinkle sesame seeds on top.)

Bake at 375° for 10-12 minutes or until golden brown. Good with soup.

SOUPS & SANDWICHES

BAKED CHICKEN SANDWICHES

1 — 3 oz. pkg. cream cheese, softened
2 Tbsp. milk
2 cups finely chopped cooked chicken
½ tsp. salt
½ tsp. pepper
2 — 8 oz. cans refrigerated crescent dinner rolls
6 Tbsp. butter, melted
1½ cups croutons, crushed

SERVES 8
Combine cheese and milk; beat until smooth. Stir in chicken, salt, and pepper.

Separate roll dough into triangles. Place 2-3 tablespoons chicken mixture on each of 8 triangles, spreading to within ½ inch of edges; moisten edges of dough with water. Place remaining 8 triangles on top; press edges to seal. Brush each sandwich with butter; sprinkle with crushed croutons. Place on lightly greased baking sheets; bake at 350° for 20-25 minutes or until lightly browned.

This is good with a salad for a light, quick meal.

ZESTY HAM SPREAD

1 cup finely chopped, cooked ham
1 cup shredded colby cheese
3 Tbsp. finely chopped green bell pepper
1 Tbsp. chopped fresh parsley
½ cup mayonnaise or salad dressing
¼ cup sour cream
2 Tbsp. prepared mustard
½ tsp. Worcestershire sauce

MAKES 1½ CUPS
In a medium bowl, combine all ingredients and mix well. Spread on Kaiser buns or slices of homemade bread for sandwiches.

This is a great recipe for using leftover holiday ham. Also good on crackers as an appetizer.

BERTA'S CHILI CUPS

1 — 8 oz. can refrigerated
   biscuits
1½ lbs. ground beef
1 medium onion, chopped
1 — 15 oz. can chili beans
1 — 15 oz. can Hunt's
   Mexican Manwich

GARNISH:
Shredded Cheddar cheese
Chopped lettuce
Chopped tomato
Sour cream
Picante sauce

SERVES 8-10
Turn a 12-tin muffin tin upside down. Spray with non-stick spray. Separate and shape biscuit dough over cups and bake at 375° for about 10 minutes or until lightly browned.

In the meantime, brown ground beef and onion in a skillet over medium high heat. Drain. Add chili beans and Manwich sauce.

Remove cooled biscuit cups from muffin tins. Fill with meat mixture. Garnish with shredded cheese, lettuce, tomato, sour cream, or picante. Serve immediately.

These easy main-dish meat cups are as pretty as they are good! Easily doubled for a crowd.

FRITOLE

French bread
Refried beans
Monterey Jack cheese
Sliced pickled jalapeno
   peppers

Slice French bread (about 1½ inch slices). Cover liberally with refried beans. Cover beans with thin slices of cheese and dot with several jalapeno rings. Place under broiler until cheese melts.

This is the simplest lunch recipe...it is fast, filling, delicious, and is great by itself or with a bowl of soup.

SOUPS & SANDWICHES

CRABMEAT CROISSANTS

½ cup mayonnaise
¼ tsp. dried dill weed
½ tsp. garlic powder
¼ cup minced fresh
  parsley
⅛ tsp. cayenne pepper
⅔ lb. crabmeat
1 cup shredded Cheddar
  cheese
1 cup shredded Monterey
  Jack cheese
1 — 2¼ oz. can sliced ripe
  black olives
4 large croissants

SERVES 8
In a medium bowl, combine mayonnaise, dill, garlic powder, parsley, cayenne pepper, crabmeat, cheese, and sliced olives. Cover and refrigerate at least one hour to allow flavors to blend. Split croissants horizontally. Spread each half with crab mixture. Place on baking sheet and broil 3-4 minutes or until heated through.

BAKED CRABMEAT SANDWICH

1 egg, slightly beaten
1 — 3 oz. pkg. cream
  cheese, softened
1 tsp. lemon juice
2 Tbsp. Parmesan cheese
2 Tbsp. chopped fresh
  parsley
3 Tbsp. mayonnaise
½ cup cooked crabmeat
3 English muffins, split
6 tomato slices

SERVES 6
Combine egg, cream cheese, lemon juice, cheese, parsley, and mayonnaise. Mix well. Stir in crabmeat; set aside. Place a tomato slice on each English muffin half. Spread crab mixture evenly over tomato slices. Broil sandwiches until golden brown.
Serve with a fresh fruit salad for a tasty luncheon.

PIZZA LOAF

½ lb. Italian sausage
½ tsp. garlic powder
1 medium onion, chopped
1 — 1 lb. can crushed
  Italian tomatoes
1 — 2 Tbsp. tomato paste
1 Tbsp. dried basil
1 tsp. dried oregano
Salt and pepper to taste
½ lb. Mozzarella cheese,
  grated
¼ lb. Cheddar cheese,
  grated
1 long loaf French bread,
  unsliced

SERVES 4-6

Brown Italian sausage in skillet. Remove with slotted spoon and drain well. In same skillet, saute garlic and onions until soft. Add tomatoes, tomato paste, and herbs. Simmer for 10-15 minutes. Add more tomato paste if necessary to make sauce thick.

Slice off top of loaf of bread lengthwise. Scoop out center of bread leaving a 1 inch shell. Place sausage/sauce mixture in shell, topping with cheeses. Press down firmly. Replace top of loaf. Wrap twice in heavy aluminum foil. Bake at 300° for 1½ hours. Remove and let set for 20 minutes. Cut in 2 inch slices to serve.

Options: Add sauteed mushrooms, peppers or chopped olives to the sausage mixture for a variation.

HAMBURGERS WITH SAVORY SAUCE

1 lb. lean ground beef
½ cup mayonnaise
2 Tbsp. Worcestershire
  sauce
½ tsp. Tabasco sauce
¼ tsp. dried savory
¼ cup ketchup
⅛ tsp. garlic salt
⅛ tsp. celery salt
4 hamburger buns,
  buttered and toasted

SERVES 4

Shape ground beef into 4 patties and broil or grill to desired doneness. In the meantime, blend mayonnaise, Worcestershire, Tabasco, ketchup, and spices. Whisk to make a smooth sauce. Place cooked patties on buns and spoon sauce over each. Can add lettuce, tomato, onion, etc., if desired, but these are delicious plain.

SOUPS & SANDWICHES

PORK SANDWICHES DELUXE

4 lb. pork roast
½ tsp. garlic salt
1 tsp. cumin
2 Tbsp. paprika
1 tsp. salt
1 tsp. pepper
1 Tbsp. salad oil
4 medium onions, thinly
   sliced
1 pkg. radishes, thinly
   sliced
Hot bottled peppers, thinly
   sliced
Bottled Italian dressing
Butter
French rolls

SERVES 12
Mix garlic salt, cumin, paprika, salt, pepper, and salad oil to form a paste. Spread over pork roast. Cover with foil and bake at 350° until golden brown (about 3-4 hours). Cool. Cut in slices.

Place cut onions, radishes, and hot peppers (to taste) in a bowl. Add salt and pepper. Marinate in Italian dressing about 2 hours. Drain.

Split French rolls. Butter each side, add pork, then salad. This is really a different sandwich...try cooking the pork roast for supper, then using the leftovers for these sandwiches the next day!

HEARTY ROAST BEEF SANDWICHES

⅓ cup sour cream
2 Tbsp. Dijon mustard
2 tsp. prepared
   horseradish
4 individual French loaves
4 slices of Provolone
   cheese, halved
1-2 lbs. thinly sliced
   cooked roast beef
1 cup alfalfa sprouts,
   optional

SERVES 4
Combine sour cream, mustard, and horseradish. Split bread loaves in half horizontally, and spread sour cream mixture on cut surfaces. Top bread bottoms with cheese and roast beef. Replace bread tops, and wrap sandwiches in aluminum foil. Bake at 350° for 25 minutes.

When done, add alfalfa sprouts if desired to warmed sandwiches. Cut each sandwich in half to serve.

56

FLANK STEAK SANDWICHES

2 flank steaks, about 1 lb. each
Seasoned salt or garlic salt
Lemon pepper

DRESSING:
1 — 8 oz. carton sour cream
½ tsp. dried dill weed
¼ cup chopped green onion

VEGETABLE TOSS:
½ cup vegetable oil
½ cup dry white wine
2 Tbsp. vinegar
2 tsp. sugar
1 tsp. dried basil
½ tsp. salt
1 pint fresh mushrooms, sliced
2 large tomatoes, coarsely chopped
½ cup sliced green onions
8 oz. fresh spinach, torn
8 — 6 inch flour tortillas

SERVES 8

Sprinkle each side of the flank steak with salt and pepper. Rub into the meat. Let stand 30 minutes. Grill over medium hot fire to desired doneness, about 5 minutes per side for medium rare. Cover and chill in refrigerator 3 to 24 hours.

Combine dressing ingredients and mix well. Cover and chill 3-24 hours. Combine first six ingredients of the vegetable toss in a jar. Cover and shake. Pour over mushrooms, tomatoes, green onions. Before serving, toss vegetable mixture with spinach. Before serving, thinly slice beef into bite-size strips. For each sandwich, spread some dressing on one side of the flour tortilla. Place some sliced beef and vegetable toss on one half of tortilla and fold.

This recipe is easy and delicious. The different parts may be done early in the day, and when ready to serve, let guests put their own sandwiches together.

SOUPS & SANDWICHES

SMOKED SAUSAGE SANDWICHES

1 lb. smoked sausage
¼ cup orange juice
1 tsp. oregano
1 red onion, quartered
2 green bell peppers,
  seeded and cut into
  ½ inch thick strips
4 pita bread rounds, cut in
  half
½ cup colby cheese, grated
½ cup Monterey jack
  cheese, grated
Hot mustard

SERVES 4

Diagonal cut smoked sausage into 30 half-inch thick pieces. Combine orange juice and oregano in a small bowl. Stir well. Separate layers of red onion quarters. Skewer sausage, onion, and bell pepper alternately. Brush with orange juice mixture.

Place skewers on grill and cook, covered, over moderate heat until vegetables are crisp-tender, and sausage is heated through. Baste with orange juice while cooking. Warm pita halves on grill toward end of cooking time.

When done, slide kabob pieces into pita pockets. Sprinkle tops with cheese and serve with hot, spicy mustard for dipping.

OPEN-FACE SANDWICHES

1 Tbsp. mustard with
  horseradish
2 Tbsp. mayonnaise
1 tsp. sesame seeds
1 — 10 oz. pkg. frozen
  broccoli spears
4 slices rye bread, toasted
4 slices lean cooked ham
4 tomato slices (optional)
4 slices purple onion
  (optional)
4 slices American cheese

SERVES 4

Combine mustard, mayonnaise, and sesame seeds. Cook broccoli according to package directions. Drain and set aside.

Spread mayonnaise mixture evenly over bread slices. Place one slice ham on each slice of bread. Add tomato and onion if desired. Arrange broccoli over this; top with cheese. Broil until cheese melts.

WAGON WHEEL SANDWICH

1 — 8 inch round loaf
   sourdough bread
2 tsp. prepared
   horseradish
¼ lb. shaved roast beef
2 Tbsp. mayonnaise
4 slices Swiss cheese
2 Tbsp. Dijon mustard
¼ lb. shaved ham
1 medium tomato, thinly
   sliced
4 slices bacon, cooked and
   drained
4 slices American cheese
½ medium-size red onion,
   thinly sliced
¼ cup butter or margarine,
   softened
1 Tbsp. sesame seeds,
   toasted
⅛ tsp. onion powder

SERVES 8

Slice bread horizontally into 6 equal layers using an electric or serrated knife. Spread horseradish on first layer, top with roast beef and second layer. Spread mayonnaise on second layer and top with Swiss cheese and third layer. Spread mustard on third layer, top with ham and fourth layer. Cover fourth layer with tomato slices, bacon and fifth bread layer. Top fifth layer with American cheese, onion, and remaining bread layer.

Combine butter, sesame seeds, and onion powder. Spread over top and sides of loaf. Place loaf on baking sheet; bake, uncovered at 400° for 15 minutes. Slice (with an electric or serrated knife) into wedges to serve.

The perfect sandwich for the big mouths in your family!

BREADS

BREADS

BANANA BLUEBERRY BREAD

½ cup shortening
1 cup sugar
2 eggs
1 cup mashed bananas
½ cup quick oats
½ cup chopped pecans
1½ cups flour
¼ tsp. salt
1 tsp. baking soda
1 cup fresh, frozen, or
    canned blueberries,
    drained

MAKES 1 LOAF
Cream shortening; add sugar gradually, beating until light and fluffy. Add eggs, beating well after each addition. Blend in mashed banana. In another bowl, combine remaining ingredients, stirring gently. Blend the two mixtures, stirring until moist. Spoon batter into a greased loaf pan. Bake at 350° for 50-55 minutes. Cool in pan for 10 minutes; remove to a wire rack.

PLUM GOOD BREAD

2 cups flour
¾ cup sugar
1 Tbsp. baking powder
1 tsp. salt
½ tsp. baking soda
½ tsp. cinnamon
1 cup quick oats
32 oz. canned purple
    plums, drained and
    chopped
2 eggs, well beaten
1 cup milk
¼ cup salad oil

MAKES 1 LOAF
Mix flour, sugar, baking powder, salt, baking soda and cinnamon. Add oats and plums, stirring to coat. In separate bowl, blend eggs, milk and oil. Add to flour mixture, stirring just until moist. Pour into greased loaf pan and bake at 350° for 1 hour or until done. Cool in pan for 10 minutes before removing.

CRANBERRY NUT BREAD

2 cups flour
1 cup sugar
1 tsp. salt
1½ tsp. baking powder
½ tsp. baking soda
1 Tbsp. lemon or orange
    peel
2 Tbsp. shortening
¾ cup orange juice
1 egg, well beaten
½ cup chopped nuts
1 cup whole cranberries,
    finely chopped

MAKES 1 LOAF
Combine all ingredients and mix well. Pour into greased loaf pan and bake at 350° for 50 minutes or until bread tests done. Freezes well.

This is a great Christmas morning treat.

APRICOT NUT BREAD

1½ cups apricot nectar
¾ cup raisins
¾ cup diced dried apricots
1 Tbsp. fresh lemon juice
¾ cup sugar
1 egg
1 Tbsp. butter, melted
2 cups flour
2 tsp. baking soda
½ tsp. salt
½ cup chopped pecans
⅓ cup milk

MAKES 1 LOAF
Combine nectar, raisins, apricots, and lemon juice in a saucepan. Cook over medium-low heat for 5 minutes. Cool. In a large bowl, combine sugar, egg, and butter, beating well. Stir in flour, soda, salt, and nuts. Add apricot mixture and mix well. Stir in milk. Pour into greased loaf pan and bake at 350° for 1 hour.

BREADS

OATMEAL RAISIN BREAD

1 cup quick oats
½ cup raisins
1 cup boiling water
4 Tbsp. butter, softened
2 cups firmly packed
   brown sugar
2 eggs
1 cup flour
1 tsp. cinnamon
1 tsp. cloves
1 tsp. baking soda
1 cup chopped pecans
Powdered sugar

MAKES 1 LARGE LOAF OR 2 SMALL LOAVES
Combine oats and raisins in a bowl. Pour boiling water over them and set aside until cool, about 15 minutes.

Meanwhile, in a large bowl, cream together the butter and brown sugar, then beat in the eggs, one at a time. Blend in the flour, spices, and baking soda. Beat in the oat/raisin mixture; fold in the pecans.

Pour the batter into greased and floured loaf pan (or 2 small ones) and bake at 350° for 45-50 minutes or until bread tests done. Cool in pan for 10 minutes, then remove. Cool completely, then dust with powdered sugar.

This rich, moist bread is great at mid-morning with coffee.

CARROT BREAD

2 eggs
1 cup sugar
½ cup oil
1½ cups flour
1 tsp. baking powder
½ tsp. salt
1 tsp. cinnamon
1 cup shredded carrots

MAKES 1 LOAF
In a large bowl, beat eggs. Gradually add sugar, beating until thick. Add oil slowly and continue beating until well mixed. Mix dry ingredients together and stir into egg mixture. Add carrots and stir until blended. Pour batter into greased and floured bread pan. Bake at 350° for 50 minutes or until bread tests done.

APPLESAUCE SPICE MUFFINS

1 cup margarine, softened
2 cups sugar
2 eggs
2 cups applesauce
4 cups flour
2 tsp. baking soda
1 tsp. salt
1 Tbsp. cinnamon
2 tsp. allspice
½ tsp. cloves
1 cup chopped pecans,
   optional

MAKES 4 DOZEN

Cream butter, gradually adding sugar. Beat well. Add eggs and beat well. Mix in applesauce.

Combine dry ingredients and stir into applesauce mixture. Add pecans if desired. Fill greased or lined muffin tins three-fourths full and bake at 350° for 15 minutes. Batter will keep in the refrigerator for two weeks.

These delicious muffins are so easy and make great breakfast treats or after-school snacks.

BREAKFAST MUFFINS

2¼ cups flour
⅓ cup sugar
1 Tbsp. baking powder
½ tsp. baking soda
¼ tsp. salt
¼ cup butter
1 cup plain yogurt
⅓ cup milk
2 eggs
1 tsp. vanilla
Preserves of your choice:
   strawberry, peach,
   apricot, blueberry,
   raspberry, etc.
Powdered sugar

MAKES 1 DOZEN

Mix dry ingredients. Melt butter, add yogurt and milk until smooth. Beat in egg and vanilla. Add to dry ingredients. Mix well. Fill greased or lined muffin tins half full with batter. Spoon preserves on batter and top with more batter. Bake at 425° 15-20 minutes or until golden brown. Sift powdered sugar on top.

BREADS

FRESH BLUEBERRY MUFFINS

1 cup blueberries
2 cups flour
¾ cup sugar
1½ tsp. baking powder
Pinch of salt
3 oz. cream cheese
2 tsp. lemon juice
½ cup milk
¼ cup butter, melted
2 eggs
2 tsp. vanilla

MAKES 2 DOZEN
Toss blueberries with 2 tablespoons flour. Set aside. Combine remaining dry ingredients; set aside.

Blend cream cheese, lemon juice, milk and butter. Add eggs and vanilla, and beat well. Add dry ingredients and stir to blend. Stir in blueberries. Fill greased muffin cups ⅔ full. Bake at 400° 18-20 minutes.

CHERRY MUFFINS

2 cups flour
⅓ cup sugar
⅓ cup maraschino
   cherries, quartered
1 Tbsp. baking powder
½ tsp. salt
¾ cup buttermilk
¼ cup vegetable oil
4 Tbsp. cherry juice
1 egg, beaten
1 tsp. almond extract
4 Tbsp. almonds, finely
   chopped
3 Tbsp. sugar

MAKES 1 DOZEN
In large mixing bowl, combine flour, sugar, cherries, baking powder and salt. In separate bowl, mix buttermilk, oil, cherry juice, egg and almond extract. Make a well in dry ingredients and stir in liquid just to moisten. Fill greased muffin cups ⅔ full. Combine almonds and remaining sugar and sprinkle over batter. Bake at 350° for 25-30 minutes. Cool 10 minutes before removing from muffin tins.

CHOCOLATE CHIP BANANA MUFFINS

½ cup butter, softened
1 cup light brown sugar,
  packed
2 eggs, lightly beaten
2 cups flour
½ tsp. salt
½ tsp. baking powder
¾ tsp. soda
2 cups ripe bananas,
  mashed (about 3)
¾ cup chopped nuts
¾ cup mini chocolate chips

MAKES 1 DOZEN
Cream together the butter and brown sugar. Add beaten eggs and mix well. Sift dry ingredients into mixture and stir until just moistened. Fold in nuts and chocolate chips. Fill greased muffin cups ⅔ full. Bake at 350° for 35-45 minutes or until golden brown.

LEMON RASPBERRY MUFFINS

2 cups flour
1 cup sugar
3 tsp. baking powder
½ tsp. salt
1 cup half and half
½ cup oil
1 tsp. lemon extract
2 eggs
1 cup fresh raspberries

MAKES 12-16 MUFFINS
In a large bowl, combine dry ingredients and mix well. In a small bowl, combine cream, oil, lemon extract, and eggs. Blend well. Add to dry ingredients and stir until just moistened. Carefully fold in raspberries. Fill lined or lightly greased muffin cups ¾ full. Bake at 425° for 20 minutes or until golden brown. Cool before removing from pan.

We love these as an after-school treat, though they are just as popular at breakfast!

BREADS

MORNING GLORY MUFFINS

4 cups flour
2½ cups sugar
4 tsp. baking soda
4 tsp. cinnamon
1 tsp. salt
4 cups peeled, grated
   apples
1 cup raisins
1 cup chopped pecans
1 cup shredded coconut
1 cup grated carrot
6 large eggs
2 cups vegetable oil
4 tsp. vanilla

MAKES 36
Sift flour, sugar, soda, cinnamon and salt into a large bowl. Stir in apples, raisins, pecans, coconut and carrot. Mix well.

In a blender, food processor or large bowl, combine eggs, oil and vanilla. Add to flour mixture and stir until just blended. Spoon batter into greased or lined muffin tins, filling ⅔ full. Bake at 350° for 20-25 minutes. Cool for five minutes before removing from pan.

PINEAPPLE BLUEBERRY MUFFINS

½ cup butter or margarine
1 cup sugar
1 tsp. vanilla
2 eggs.
3 cups flour
½ tsp. salt
3 tsp. baking powder
¼ tsp. baking soda
1 cup pineapple juice or
   sour cream or a
   combination of both
1⅓ cups crushed
   pineapple, well-drained
1⅓ cups blueberries

MAKES 2 DOZEN
Cream butter with sugar until light and fluffy. Beat in vanilla and eggs. Sift together 2½ cups flour and other dry ingredients. Add to butter mixture, alternating with juice or sour cream. Begin and end with dry ingredients. Stir remaining ½ cup flour into fruit. Fold floured fruit into batter. Spoon into greased or lined muffin tins. Bake at 400° for 20-25 minutes. These freeze well.

BREADS

POPPY SEED MUFFINS

2 cups flour
3 tsp. poppy seeds
¼ tsp. salt
¼ tsp. baking soda
1 cup sugar
½ cup butter or margarine
2 eggs
1 cup plain yogurt
1 tsp. vanilla

TOPPING:
¼ cup orange juice
¾ cup sugar
½ tsp. almond extract

MAKES 1 DOZEN
In a small bowl, stir together flour, poppy seeds, salt and baking soda. In large bowl, cream together sugar and butter. Beat in eggs one at a time. Stir in yogurt and vanilla until well blended. Add flour mixture and stir just until moistened. Fill greased muffin cups ⅔ full. Bake at 400° for 15-20 minutes.

Mix together orange juice, sugar, and almond extract. Drizzle each muffin with topping.

PROCESSOR MUFFINS

1½ cups flour
1 tsp. baking powder
1 tsp. soda
1 tsp. salt
½ cup pecans, optional
½ cup dates
¾ cup sugar
1 medium unpeeled
   orange, cut into eighths
   and seeded
½ cup butter or margarine
1 large egg
½ cup orange juice

MAKES 18 MUFFINS
Measure dry ingredients into bowl of food processor. Process until mixed. Add nuts and pulse 1-2 times. Remove and set aside. Process dates and sugar until dates are chopped. Add orange pieces and pulse until they are chopped fine. Add butter, egg, and orange juice. Process to blend about 25 seconds. Add dry mixture and pulse until all ingredients are moist. Spoon batter into greased or lined muffin tins and bake for 15 minutes at 400°.

BREADS

APPLE-PECAN COFFEE CAKE

½ cup shortening
½ cup butter or margarine,
   softened
2 cups sugar
2 eggs
3 cups flour
2 tsp. baking powder
1 tsp. baking soda
¼ tsp. salt
1¾ cups buttermilk
2 medium cooking apples,
   peeled and thinly sliced

TOPPING:
½ cup flour
½ cup sugar
1½ tsp. cinnamon
3 Tbsp. butter or margarine
½ cup pecans, finely
   chopped

SERVES 15

Cream shortening and butter, gradually adding sugar. Beat until light and fluffy. Add eggs, one at a time, beating well after each addition.

Combine flour, baking powder, soda, and salt; add to creamed mixture alternately with buttermilk. Spoon half of batter into a greased and floured 9 x 13 inch baking pan. Arrange apple slices over batter. Spread remaining batter over top.

Combine ½ cup flour, ½ cup sugar and cinnamon. Cut in butter until mixture resembles crumbs. Stir in chopped pecans. Sprinkle topping evenly over batter. Bake at 350° for 45 minutes. Cool before cutting into squares to serve.

BLUEBERRY CRUNCH COFFEECAKE

BATTER:
¼ cup butter or margarine, softened
¾ cup sugar
1 egg
2 cups flour
2 tsp. baking powder
¼ tsp. salt
½ cup milk
2 cups blueberries, drained

TOPPING:
½ cup sugar
⅓ cup flour
1 tsp. cinnamon
¼ cup butter or margarine, softened

SERVES 9

Mix margarine and sugar until light and fluffy. Add egg and mix well. Add dry ingredients alternately with milk until just blended. Carefully stir in blueberries.

Pour into greased 9 x 9 inch baking pan. Combine topping ingredients until mixture resembles crumbs. Sprinkle on top of batter and bake at 375° for 40-45 minutes.

This is wonderful for breakfast or as a dessert with vanilla ice cream on top of each serving.

CRANBERRY COFFEECAKE

2 cups flour
1 tsp. baking powder
1 tsp. baking soda
½ tsp. salt
½ cup butter
1 cup sugar
2 large eggs
1 tsp. almond extract
1 cup sour cream
8 oz. whole cranberry sauce
½ cup chopped almonds
Powdered sugar

SERVES 8-10

Sift together flour, baking powder, soda, and salt. In a large bowl, beat ½ cup butter and sugar until fluffy. Add eggs, beating well after each addition. Mix in extract. Stir in dry ingredients alternately with sour cream. Spoon ½ batter into greased tube or Bundt pan. Add ½ cranberry sauce and swirl through batter. Spoon remaining batter evenly over the top and then spoon on remaining cranberry sauce. Sprinkle with almonds. Cool 15 minutes before serving. Sprinkle with powdered sugar.

BREADS

BLUEBERRY POPPY SEED CAKE

CAKE:
⅔ cup sugar
½ cup margarine, softened
2 tsp. grated lemon peel
1 egg
1½ cups flour
2 Tbsp. poppy seed
½ tsp. baking soda
¼ tsp. salt
½ cup sour cream

FILLING:
2 cups blueberries, drained
  (fresh, frozen, or
  canned)
⅓ cup sugar
2 tsp. flour
¼ tsp. nutmeg

GLAZE:
⅓ cup powdered sugar
1 or 2 tsp. milk

SERVES 8

In a large bowl, beat sugar and margarine until light and fluffy. Add lemon peel and egg, beating well. Combine dry ingredients and add to margarine mixture alternately with sour cream. Spread batter over bottom and 1 inch up sides of a greased and floured 9 or 10 inch springform pan. Make sure batter on sides is ¼ inch thick.

Combine all filling ingredients and spoon over batter. Bake at 350° for 45-55 minutes or until crust is golden brown. Cool slightly before removing sides of pan.

In a small bowl, combine powdered sugar and milk for desired consistency. Drizzle over cake. Serve warm or cool.

CINDY'S CREAM CHEESE COFFEE CAKE

2 pkg. crescent rolls
2 — 8 oz. pkg. cream
  cheese, softened
¾ cup sugar
1 tsp. lemon juice
1 tsp. vanilla
1 egg yolk, save white
Chopped almonds

Lightly grease a 9 x 13 inch pan. Line bottom of pan with one package of rolls. Mix cream cheese, sugar, lemon juice, vanilla, and egg yolk and pour over roll dough. Layer second package of rolls on top of cream cheese mixture. Pinch edges of rolls together. Brush slightly beaten egg white on roll dough and sprinkle with almonds. Bake at 350° for 30-40 minutes.

CHERRY CHEESE COFFEE CAKE

1½ cups flour
1 cup quick oats
¾ cup sugar
¾ cup margarine
½ cup sour cream
1 egg
½ tsp. baking soda
1 — 8 oz. pkg. cream
   cheese, softened
¼ cup sugar
¼ tsp. almond extract
1 egg
¾ cup cherry pie filling
⅓ cup sliced almonds

10 SERVINGS

Mix together flour, oats, and ¾ cup sugar in a large bowl. Cut in margarine until mixture resembles crumbs. Reserve 1 cup.

Add sour cream, one egg and soda to remaining crumb mixture and mix well. Spread onto bottom and 2 inches up sides of greased 9 inch springform pan. Beat cream cheese, ¼ cup sugar and extract until well blended. Blend in 1 egg. Pour into crust. Top with pie filling. Sprinkle with reserved crumb mixture and almonds.

Bake 50-55 minutes or until golden brown at 350°. Cool 15 minutes before removing rim of pan.

Try this for Christmas brunch…it is sure to be a hit!

BREADS

GRAN'S SOUR CREAM COFFEE CAKE

½ lb. margarine, melted
2 cups sugar
2 eggs
1 tsp. vanilla
2 cups flour
1 tsp. baking powder
1 cup sour cream
⅛ tsp. salt

TOPPING:
3 Tbsp. brown sugar
½ Tbsp. cinnamon
½ cup pecans, finely
   chopped

Mix margarine and sugar until well-blended. Add eggs and vanilla, and mix well. Mix in dry ingredients, then sour cream and salt until well blended.

Grease and flour a Bundt pan. Pour ½ batter in pan. Sprinkle with half of the topping mixture. Add remainder of the batter, then sprinkle with the rest of the topping mixture. Bake for 1 hour at 325° or until cake tests done.

CHEESE BREAD

3 cups Bisquick
1 cup milk
2 eggs
2 heaping Tbsp. Parmesan
   cheese
1 cup butter, melted
1 cup sugar
1 cup sour cream
Sesame seeds
Parmesan cheese

SERVES 10-12
Add milk to Bisquick and mix well. Add eggs and blend. Combine cheese and butter; stir into Bisquick mixture. Add sugar and mix. Add sour cream and mix again. Pour batter into generously greased 9 x 13 inch pan. Sprinkle sesame seeds on top. Sprinkle additional Parmesan cheese on top. Bake at 350° for 40-45 minutes or until golden brown.

This is a wonderfully easy bread that is a nice change from cornbread...goes great with chili or soup.

CLOUD BISCUITS

2 cups flour, sifted
1 Tbsp. sugar
3 tsp. baking powder
½ tsp. salt
½ tsp. cream of tartar
½ cup shortening
1 egg, beaten
⅔ cup milk

MAKES 1 DOZEN

Mix dry ingredients in a bowl. Cut in shortening until mixture resembles crumbs. Combine egg and milk and add to flour mixture all at once. Stir until dough follows fork around bowl. Turn onto lightly floured surface, knead about 20 strokes gently with heel of hand. Roll dough to ¾ inch thickness. Cut with 2 inch cutter without twisting. Place on cookie sheet. Bake at 450° for 10-14 minutes.

These delicious biscuits are easy enough for kids to make...make them a habit at mealtime!

HOEDOWN BISCUITS

1½ cups flour
½ cup yellow cornmeal
2 tsp. baking powder
¼ tsp. baking soda
¼ tsp. salt
½ cup butter or margarine
½ cup shredded Cheddar
    cheese
½ cup buttermilk
1 — 4 oz. can diced green
    chilies

MAKES 1 DOZEN

Stir together the dry ingredients. Cut in butter until mixture resembles crumbs. Stir in cheese. Make a well in center of mixture.

Stir together buttermilk and un-drained chilies. Add to well in center of dry ingredients. Stir just until moistened. Turn dough onto a lightly floured surface. Knead quickly 10 or 12 strokes. Pat to ½ inch thickness. Cut with biscuit cutter. Place on un-greased baking sheet and bake at 450° for 12-15 minutes.

BREADS

CHUCKWAGON SOURDOUGH BISCUITS

STARTER:
1 pkg. dry yeast
2 cups warm water
2 cups flour

BISCUIT DOUGH:
2 cups flour
1 Tbsp. sugar
1 Tbsp. baking powder
⅓ cup shortening
1 tsp. salt
2 cups starter

MAKES 2 DOZEN

Combine starter ingredients in large bowl (not metal). Mix well and let stand, covered loosely with plastic wrap, at room temperature for 48 hours. To store starter, refrigerate in a jar with a loose-fitting lid. When making biscuits, stir starter well, pour out required amount and replenish starter with 1 cup flour, 1 cup milk, ⅓ cup sugar. Replenish at least once a week.

To make biscuits, combine dry ingredients in a bowl. Cut in shortening until mixture resembles crumbs. Stir in starter and blend. Knead lightly. Roll out and cut for biscuits. Place on lightly greased cookie sheet and let rise for one hour. Bake 10-12 minutes at 400° or until lightly browned.
We cook these in a Dutch oven at the chuckwagon during branding time...the cowboys say they've never tasted better biscuits!

CALIENTE CORNBREAD

1 cup cornmeal
½ cup flour
½ tsp. salt
1 cup milk
2 eggs
½ cup oil or bacon
  drippings
¾ tsp. soda
1 — 16 oz. can creamed
  corn
1 onion, chopped
½ lb. Cheddar cheese,
  grated
3 jalapeno peppers,
  chopped, or 1 — 4 oz.
  can chopped green
  chilies

SERVES 10-12
Mix all ingredients until well blended. Grease an 11 x 16 inch jelly roll pan. Sprinkle with cornmeal. Pour batter into prepared pan and bake at 400° until browned, about 30 minutes.

This rich, flavorful cornbread is great with a side dish of beans for a simple, honest meal.

APPLESAUCE DROP DONUTS

2 cups flour
½ cup sugar
2 tsp. baking powder
½ tsp. salt
1 tsp. cinnamon
1 egg
½ cup applesauce
½ cup milk
1½ Tbsp. oil
Oil for deep frying
Sugar/cinnamon mixture

MAKES 4 DOZEN
Combine dry ingredients in a large bowl. Add beaten egg, applesauce, milk, and oil. Stir to blend. Drop by teaspoonfuls into hot oil (375°). Fry to golden brown. Drain and roll in sugar/cinnamon mixture while warm.

This is a good after-school snack, or weekend breakfast treat. If you don't have a deep fat fryer, pour oil in a small saucepan to about a 4 inch depth, and fry donuts about 3 at a time.

BREADS

NUTMEG DONUT DROPS

3 cups flour
⅔ cup sugar
4 tsp. baking powder
1 tsp. salt
1 tsp. nutmeg
1 cup milk
4 Tbsp. oil
1 tsp. vanilla
2 eggs
Oil for deep frying
Sugar

MAKES 4 DOZEN

Mix first five ingredients in a bowl. Stir in milk, oil, vanilla, and eggs until well blended. Drop by teaspoonfuls into hot oil, about 375°. Roll drops in sugar while still warm.

These are so good and easy…the kids just love them. If you have a Fry Daddy cooker, you will avoid the mess of deep fat frying, while enjoying the delicious results…it is a great invention.

BUTTERHORNS

2 cups sifted flour
1 cup butter, softened
1 egg yolk
¾ cup sour cream
¾ cup sugar
1 tsp. cinnamon
½ cup finely chopped nuts

GLAZE:
1 cup powdered sugar
2 Tbsp. butter, softened
¼ cup half and half

MAKES 3 DOZEN

Mix together flour and butter. Blend in egg yolk and sour cream. Divide dough into three equal portions. Wrap each in plastic and refrigerate at least 2 hours.

Combine sugar, cinnamon, and nuts. Roll each portion of dough into an 8-inch circle. Sprinkle with ⅓ of the sugar/cinnamon mixture. Cut into wedges. Roll up each wedge, starting at the wide end. Place point-side down on a greased baking sheet. Bake at 350° for 20-25 minutes. Cool. Combine glaze ingredients and drizzle on cooked butterhorns.

These fancy little pastries make a brunch or morning coffee extra special!

BREAKFAST BUTTERSCOTCH ROLLS

15-18 Rhodes frozen
   dinner rolls
1 — 3 oz. pkg. butterscotch
   pudding
⅔ cup brown sugar
½ cup chopped nuts
½ cup butter or margarine,
   melted

MAKES 1½ DOZEN

Grease bundt or 9 x 13 inch pan. Place frozen rolls in pan. Mix pudding, brown sugar and nuts. Sprinkle on rolls. Pour melted butter on top. Cover and set on counter overnight. First thing in the morning, bake rolls at 350° for 35 minutes (cover for first 20 minutes). Remove from oven and turn out on serving dish. Allow time for all the yummy butterscotch syrup to drizzle down!

GERMAINE'S GERMAN DUMPLINGS (MAULDASHA)

DOUGH:
3 eggs
½ cup lukewarm water
Flour to make a fairly stiff
   dough

FILLING:
Fruit (your choice)
Sugar
Flour
   Or
Cottage cheese
Apple pie filling
Sugar to taste

MAKES 1 DOZEN

Combine dough ingredients in a bowl. Roll very thin and cut in 4 inch squares. Place 1 heaping tablespoon fruit in center of square. Top with 1 heaping teaspoon flour and 1 tablespoon sugar. Pull corners to center and pinch seams together to seal. Boil salt water in kettle. When water is boiling, add dumplings one at a time, keeping water boiling, until all dumplings are in kettle. Boil and let simmer for about 25 minutes. Drain; place in a bowl and top with cream and sugar or eat plain.

These traditional German dumplings are a favorite when made with "German Wonder-berries."

BREADS

BREAD STIX

¾ cup flat beer
¾ cup oil
1 pkg. yeast
¾ cup warm water
4½ cups flour
1½ tsp. salt
¾ Tbsp. fennel seed
   (optional)

TOPPING:
1 egg, beaten
Sesame seeds
   Or
Poppy seeds

Mix beer and oil. Dissolve yeast in warm water and add to liquids. Add 3½ cups flour, salt and fennel seed. Mix well. Work in last cup of flour. Let rise until double, knead down and then pull off pieces the size of an egg. Roll into sticks and place on a cookie sheet. If you choose, brush stix with beaten egg and sprinkle with sesame or poppy seeds (if you didn't put fennel in the dough.) Bake at 325° for 35 minutes.

CARAMEL BOTTOM DINNER ROLLS

1 pkg. active dry yeast
¼ cup warm water
1 cup milk, scalded
¼ cup sugar
¼ cup shortening
1 tsp. salt
3½ cups sifted flour
1 egg

CARAMEL MIXTURE:
½ cup butter or margarine
½ cup brown sugar

MAKES 2 DOZEN
Soften yeast in warm water. Combine milk, sugar, shortening, and salt; cool to lukewarm. Add half the flour and beat well. Beat in yeast and egg. Gradually add remaining flour to form soft dough, beating well. Place in greased bowl, turning once to greased surface. Cover and let rise until double.

Place butter and margarine in a 9 x 13 inch baking dish. Melt together in moderate oven or microwave. Turn out dough on lightly floured surface and shape into dinner rolls. Place rolls on top of caramel mixture. Cover and let rolls rise until double. Bake at 350° for 12-15 minutes. Cool 2-3 minutes; invert on rack; remove pan.

HOMEMADE PRETZELS

1 pkg. dry yeast
½ tsp. sugar
1½ cups warm beer
4½ cups flour
1 egg, beaten
Kosher salt

MAKES 2 DOZEN
Dissolve yeast and sugar in warm beer in large mixing bowl. Add flour and mix until blended. Turn dough out onto lightly floured surface. Knead 8-10 minutes until dough is smooth and elastic.

Place in a greased bowl, turning once. Cover and let rise until doubled. Punch down.

Using kitchen shears dipped in flour, cut dough into 24 pieces; roll each into a ball. With floured hands, roll each ball between hands to form a rope 14 inches long. Twist each into a pretzel shape, placing on greased foil-lined baking sheets, about 1½ inches apart. Brush each pretzel with egg; sprinkle with kosher salt (rock or table may be substituted). Bake at 475° for 12 to 15 minutes or until golden brown. Remove to a wire rack. Serve warm.

BREADS

APPLE CINNAMON BUNS

YEAST DOUGH:
¾ cup milk
½ cup sugar
1¼ tsp. salt
½ cup butter
⅓ cup warm water
2 pkg. yeast
5½ to 6½ cups flour
3 eggs, room temperature

FILLING:
24 oz. cream cheese,
    softened and whipped
6 peeled and grated
    Jonathan apples
2 cups sugar
4 tsp. cinnamon
4 Tbsp. flour
½ cup butter, melted

TOPPING:
2 cups brown sugar
4 Tbsp. flour
4 tsp. cinnamon
4 Tbsp. butter, melted

FROSTING:
2-3 cups powdered sugar
1-2 Tbsp. water
½ tsp. vanilla

MAKES 36 BUNS

Scald milk, stir in sugar, salt and butter. Cool to lukewarm. In a large bowl, dissolve yeast in warm water. Add milk mixture, eggs, and 5 cups flour. Mix, adding flour as needed. Knead until dough is smooth and elastic. Place in a greased bowl, turn, cover and let rise in a warm place until double in bulk. Punch dough down and divide in half. Roll each piece into an 11 x 14 inch rectangle.

Spread half of cream cheese on each dough half. Mix sugar, cinnamon, flour and apples. Put half of apple mixture atop each dough rectangle. Drizzle half of butter on each dough piece. Roll each section up from long side and seal edges firmly. Cut into 1-inch slices. Place slices on a lightly greased baking pan.

Mix topping ingredients and sprinkle on top of rolls. Cover and let rise until doubled. Bake at 400° for 15-20 minutes. Drizzle frosting over the top of hot rolls.

CORNMEAL YEAST ROLLS

¾ cup milk
1¼ cups cornmeal
1 cup boiling water
1 pkg. yeast
½ cup warm water
½ cup butter or margarine,
  melted
⅓ cup sugar
2 egg yolks, slightly beaten
2 tsp. salt
4 to 5 cups flour

MAKES 4 DOZEN
Scald milk. Cool. Combine cornmeal and 1 cup boiling water in a large bowl. Let stand 10 minutes.

Dissolve yeast in ½ cup warm water. Let stand 5 minutes. Add scalded milk, butter, sugar, egg yolks, and salt to yeast mixture. Blend well. Gradually add to cornmeal, stirring well. Gradually stir in enough flour to make a soft dough.

Turn dough out on floured surface and knead until smooth and elastic. Place in greased bowl, turn once, cover and let rise until doubled. Punch down, shape into 2½ inch balls; place on greased baking sheets. Let rise until doubled. Bake at 400° for 18-20 minutes or until golden brown.

BREADS

ORANGE CRESCENT ROLLS

1 pkg. yeast
¼ cup warm water
¼ cup sugar
1 tsp. salt
2 eggs
½ cup sour cream
6 Tbsp. butter, melted
2¾ to 3 cups flour
¾ cup sugar
2 Tbsp. grated orange rind
1 Tbsp. butter, melted

GLAZE:
¾ cup sugar
½ cup sour cream
2 Tbsp. orange juice
¼ cup butter

MAKES 2 DOZEN

Dissolve yeast in warm water in bowl. Stir in ¼ cup sugar, salt, eggs, sour cream and 6 tablespoons butter, mixing well. Gradually add 2 cups flour, beating until smooth. Knead remaining flour into dough. Let rise until doubled. Punch down and knead 15 times. Roll ½ dough into a 12 inch circle.

Combine ¾ cup sugar and grated orange rind. Brush dough with 1 tablespoon melted butter and sprinkle with ½ orange/sugar mixture. Cut into 12 wedges. Roll up, starting with the wide end. Repeat with the remaining dough. Place point side down in 3 rows in a greased 9 x 13 inch pan. Cover and let rise. Bake at 350° for 20-30 minutes until golden. Top with glaze.

Glaze: Combine ingredients and boil for 3 minutes, stirring constantly. Pour over rolls when removed from oven.

OATMEAL BREAD

1 pkg. yeast
½ cup warm water
2 cups boiling water
2 cups oatmeal
½ cup brown sugar
3 Tbsp. butter
1½ tsp. salt
5 to 6 cups flour

MAKES 2 LOAVES

Dissolve yeast in warm water. In large bowl, stir oatmeal in boiling water; add sugar, butter and salt. Let cool and add yeast. Mix in enough flour so dough can be kneaded. Knead for 10 minutes. Place back in bowl. Cover and let rise until doubled in bulk. Punch down, knead again adding more flour as necessary. Knead for 10 minutes. Shape into 2 loaves and place in greased loaf pans. Cover and let rise again. Bake at 375° for about 45 minutes. Butter top crust lightly. Remove from pans to wire rack and cool.

SOUR CREAM YEAST DOUGH

2 cups sour cream
2 pkg. dry yeast
½ cup warm water
¼ cup margarine or butter, softened
⅓ cup sugar
2 tsp. salt
2 eggs
6 cups flour

MAKES 2 LOAVES

Heat sour cream over low heat until lukewarm; stir frequently. Dissolve yeast in water in large bowl. Add warm sour cream, margarine, sugar, salt, eggs, and 2 cups flour; beat until smooth. Add enough of the remaining flour until dough cleans side of bowl. Knead until smooth. Cover, let rise in a warm place about an hour or until doubled. Punch down dough. Shape into loaves, let rise until double; bake at 375° for 30 minutes or until bread sounds hollow when tapped. Remove from pans to cool on wire rack.

BREADS

ONION TWIST

1 pkg. dry yeast
¼ cup warm water
4 cups flour
¼ cup sugar
1½ tsp. salt
½ cup hot water
½ cup milk
¼ cup margarine, softened
1 egg

FILLING:
¼ cup butter or margarine,
   softened
¼ cup dried minced onions
1 Tbsp. Parmesan cheese
1 Tbsp. poppy seeds
1 tsp. garlic salt
1 tsp. paprika

MAKES 1 LARGE LOAF
In a large bowl, dissolve yeast in warm water. Add 2 cups flour, sugar, salt, hot water, milk, margarine, and egg. Blend well. Stir in remaining flour to form a soft dough. Cover; let rise 1 hour. Punch down. Toss on a floured surface until no longer sticky. Roll dough into an 18 x 12-inch rectangle.

Combine filling ingredients and blend well. Spread filling on top of dough rectangle. Cut lengthwise into 3 strips. Fold over each strip lengthwise and seal edges and ends. Place strips on greased cookie sheet and braid together. Cover and let rise 1 hour. Bake at 350° 30-35 minutes. Can be made into 2 small loaves by cutting the strips in half, then braiding.

This tender bread would be delicious with a stew or Italian-style main course.

TUPPERWARE BREAD

9 cups flour, unsifted
1½ cups milk, scalded
1½ cups cold water
⅔ cup sugar
2 tsp. salt
4 eggs, beaten
2 pkg. dry yeast
2 sticks margarine, melted

MAKES 4 DOZEN ROLLS

Place flour in a large (6 quart) Tupperware bowl and make a well in center. Take scalded milk and add cold water to cool. Add sugar, salt, beaten eggs, and yeast to liquid. Pour into well. DO NOT MIX. Seal lid on bowl and wait until it pops off (about 30 minutes.) Add melted margarine and stir to mix. Knead to proper consistency, adding flour as needed. Seal lid on bowl again. When rising dough has popped the lid, it is ready to roll out.

Use dough for cinnamon rolls, dinner rolls, loaves, etc. Let rise before baking at 400° until browned.

This dough makes a light, tender bread and it is so easy. Can be made without the Tupperware bowl if you don't have one.

BREADS

WHOLE WHEAT POTATO ONION BREAD

1¾ cups white flour
2 pkg. yeast
1 cup milk
½ cup water
2 Tbsp. butter
2 Tbsp. sugar
1 tsp. salt
1½ cups instant mashed
    potatoes, prepared
½ cup sour cream
½ cup fresh onion, minced
2 tsp. dill seed
1 tsp. garlic powder
4-5 cups whole wheat flour
1 Tbsp. oil

MAKES 2 LOAVES

Stir together the white flour and yeast. Heat the milk, water, butter, sugar and salt over low heat until warm, stirring to blend. Add liquid mixture to the flour mixture and beat until smooth. Add the potatoes, sour cream, onion, dill seed and garlic powder; beat until smooth. Add enough of the whole wheat flour to make a moderately stiff dough. Turn out on a floured surface and let rest 4 minutes.

Knead until smooth; let rise in a covered bowl until doubled in size. Punch down. Divide the dough in half and shape into 2 loaves. Place in 2 greased loaf pans; let the dough rise until almost double. Bake at 375° for 35-40 minutes. Remove bread from pans to cool on a wire rack and brush the tops with oil.

SALADS

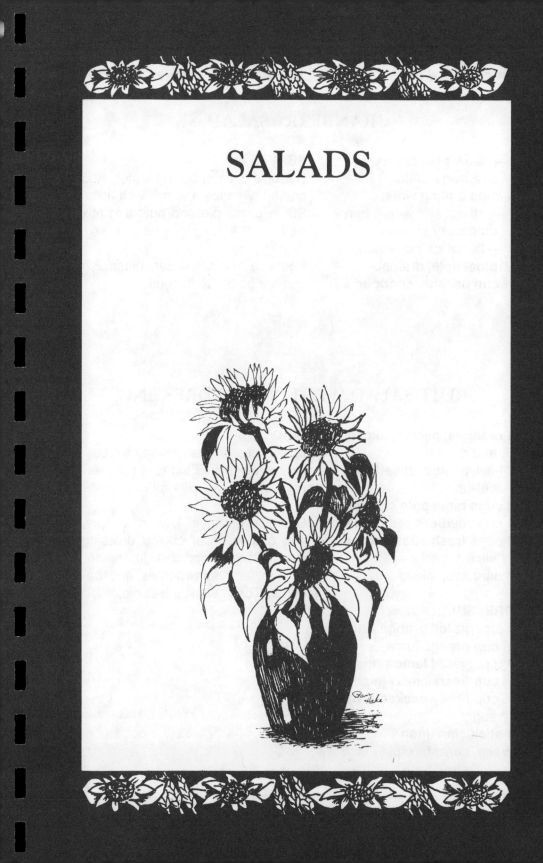

SALADS

CRANBERRY SALAD

1 — 6 oz. pkg. cherry or
   raspberry Jello
2 cups boiling water
1 — 16 oz. can whole berry
   cranberry sauce
1 — 20 oz. can crushed
   pineapple, drained
½ cup pecans, chopped

SERVES 6-8
Dissolve Jello in boiling water. Add cranberry sauce and mix with Jello. Stir in pineapple and nuts and mix well.

Pour into an 8 inch square glass dish and refrigerate to congeal.

FRUIT SALAD WITH CITRUS DRESSING

4 oranges, peeled, sliced,
   and cut-up
2 kiwi, peeled, sliced, and
   cut-up
2 cups pineapple chunks
1 cup seedless red grapes
2 cups fresh strawberries,
   sliced
3 bananas, sliced

DRESSING:
1 tsp. grated orange rind
⅔ cup orange juice
1 tsp. grated lemon rind
⅓ cup fresh lemon juice
⅓ cup firmly packed brown
   sugar
1 stick cinnamon
½ tsp. cornstarch

SERVES 6-8
In a small saucepan, combine dressing ingredients. Bring to a boil, stirring constantly. Boil 1 minute; cool.

Combine oranges, kiwi, pineapple, and grapes. Pour cooled dressing over fruit; cover and chill. Just before serving, add strawberries and bananas. Toss gently and serve.

SALADS

FROG-EYE SALAD

½ cup sugar
1 Tbsp. flour
1 tsp. salt
1 egg
1 cup pineapple juice
1¼ tsp. lemon juice
1½ quarts water
1½ tsp. cooking oil
1 — 8 oz. pkg. Acini de
  Pepe
½ cup miniature
  marshmallows
2 — 11 oz. cans Mandarin
  oranges, drained
1 — 20 oz. can pineapple
  chunks, drained
1 — 10 oz. can crushed
  pineapple, drained
1 — 8 oz. carton whipped
  topping
½ cup coconut

SERVES 12

Combine sugar, flour and ½ teaspoon salt. Gradually stir in the egg and pineapple juice. Cook mixture over moderate heat, stirring until thick. Add lemon juice and cool to room temperature. Bring the water, remaining salt and the oil to a boil. Add the Acini de Pepe and cook at a full boil until done. Drain and rinse. Rinse again and drain well. Cool to room temperature. Combine egg mixture and Acini de Pepe by mixing lightly, but thoroughly. Refrigerate overnight in airtight container. Add remaining ingredients and mix lightly. Chill in airtight container for up to a week if necessary.

This is a great salad to take to family reunions or potluck suppers.

DOUBLE LEMON SALAD

2 — 3 oz. pkg. lemon Jello
2 cups boiling water
½ cup cold water
1 — 14 oz. can lemon pie
  filling
1 — 14 oz. can crushed
  pineapple, undrained
1 cup sour cream
3 Tbsp. powdered sugar

SERVES 12

In a bowl, dissolve Jello in boiling water; add cold water. Add pie filling, and whisk until well blended. Stir in pineapple until mixed. Pour into a 9 x 13 inch dish and chill until set. Blend sour cream and powdered sugar, pour on top of Jello. Chill.

This unusual Jello salad makes a good dessert, too. Serve with sugar cookies, or halve it and pour into a baked pie shell.

SALADS

ORANGE TAPIOCA SALAD

2 — 3 oz. pkg. vanilla
  tapioca pudding
1 — 3 oz. pkg. orange Jello
3 cups hot water
1 — 12 oz. carton Cool
  Whip
1 — 6 oz. can Mandarin
  oranges drained
1 — 16 oz. can crushed
  pineapple, drained

SERVES 6-8
Combine pudding mix, Jello and water in a saucepan. Bring to boil, stirring gently. Boil until thick. Cool until
warm. Add Cool Whip and mix well.
Fold in drained fruit. Pour into mold
or 8 inch square dish and refrigerate
for at least 2 hours before serving.

INDIVIDUAL FROZEN FRUIT SALAD

2 cups sour cream
2 Tbsp. lemon juice
½ cup sugar
⅛ tsp. salt
1 — 8 oz. can crushed
  pineapple, drained
1 banana, diced
¼ cup pecans, chopped
4 drops red food coloring
1 — 16 oz. can pitted bing
  cherries, drained

SERVES 12
Combine all ingredients and spoon
into paper-cup lined muffin tins.
Cover with plastic wrap and freeze.
Remove 15 minutes before serving,
peel paper from each salad, and
transfer to a bed of lettuce.

WALDORF SALAD

2 cups apples, diced and
  unpared (use a
  combination of red and
  green)
1 cup celery, diced
⅓ cup pecans, chopped
½ cup raisins
½ cup Miracle Whip

SERVES 4
Combine ingredients and toss. For a
variation, add green grapes. For a
light version, substitute the Miracle
Whip with a combination of 1 tablespoon apple juice, 1 tablespoon
plain nonfat yogurt, and 1 tablespoon reduced-calorie mayonnaise.

SALADS

QUICK FRUIT SALAD

1 — 16 oz. can sliced
  apricots, drained
1 — 16 oz. can sliced
  pears, drained
1 — 11 oz. can Mandarin
  oranges, drained
1 — 14 oz. can pineapple
  chunks, drained
1 — 21 oz. can peach pie
  filling (can substitute
  apricot or cherry)
2 bananas
Cool Whip

SERVES 6-8
Mix the fruits together. Stir in pie filling. Just before serving, add the bananas, and top with Cool Whip.

Try using all fresh fruits when in season, or add fresh strawberries and grapes to the listed ingredients when available. This versatile salad begs for your own touches...what is listed is just a place to start!

SUMMER'S BEST FRUIT SALAD

1 cup strawberries, cut up
1 cup fresh pineapple,
  cut up
1 cup seedless green
  grapes
1 cup seedless red grapes
1 or 2 oranges, peeled and
  sectioned
1 cup apples, diced
1 banana, sliced
1 — 16 oz. can sliced
  peaches or fruit cocktail,
  drain and reserve juice
⅓ pkg. (3.5 oz.) instant
  vanilla pudding

SERVES 6
Combine all fruit in a large bowl. Combine pudding with juice from canned fruit. Pour pudding mix over the fruit and mix. Chill and serve.

Too easy and good to be true!

SALADS

DIVINE FRUIT SALAD

12 oz. frozen berries
(blueberries,
raspberries,
strawberries, or a
mixture of all three)
½ cup IMO
¼ cup sugar
2 tsp. poppy seeds
2 — 11 oz. cans Mandarin
oranges, drained
1 — 20 oz. can pineapple
chunks, drained

SERVES 6
Puree 1 cup berries, IMO, sugar, and poppy seeds. Mix remaining berries, oranges, and pineapple chunks in a bowl. Pour the puree mixture over and mix together. Chill for 1 hour and serve.

IMO is lightly sweetened sour cream, available in your supermarket dairy case.

STRAWBERRY PRETZEL SALAD

2 cups pretzels, coarsely
crushed
¾ cup melted butter
3 Tbsp. sugar
8 oz. cream cheese,
softened
1 cup sugar
9 oz. Cool Whip
2 — 3 oz. pkgs. strawberry
Jello
2 cups boiling water
20 oz. frozen strawberries

SERVES 10-12
Combine pretzels with melted butter and sugar. Spread in the bottom of a 9 x 13 inch pan. Bake 8-10 minutes at 400° and cool to room temperature.

Blend softened cream cheese and 1 cup sugar, then fold in Cool Whip. Spread this mixture on the cooled crust. Dissolve Jello in boiling water, and stir in the frozen strawberries. When partially set, pour over the cream cheese layer and refrigerate until completely set.

This one will make you famous.

SALADS

APRICOT-CHEESE SALAD

1 — 15 oz. can apricots, strained and cut up (reserve juice)
1 — 15 oz. can crushed pineapple, drained (reserve juice)
1 — 3 oz. package orange Jello
1 cup boiling water
⅓ cup miniature marshmallows
⅓ cup sugar
3 Tbsp. flour
1 egg, beaten
3 Tbsp. butter
½ cup whipped cream
¾ cup grated Cheddar cheese

SERVES 10-12

Drain the juice from the two cans of fruit and save it for later in the recipe. Dissolve the Jello in the boiling water. Add ½ cup of the combined fruit juices to the Jello. Refrigerate until semi-jelled and fold in the fruit. Pour into 9 x 13 inch pan. Return to the refrigerator.

For the top layer combine sugar and flour. Blend in the egg and remaining fruit juice. Cook over medium heat until thick. Stir in butter and let cool. Fold in whipped cream and spread over Jello. Sprinkle with grated cheese.

CALIFORNIA SALAD

12 strawberries, sliced
3 kiwi, peeled and sliced
1 avocado, peeled and sliced
Bibb lettuce

ORANGE DRESSING:
⅓ cup olive oil
3 Tbsp. raspberry vinegar
3 Tbsp. orange juice (fresh is best)
½ tsp. salt
⅛ tsp. pepper

SERVES 6

On individual serving plates, arrange fruits on Bibb lettuce leaves. Top with Orange Dressing just before serving. (If you prepare these ahead of time, wait to add avocado as it will darken.)

To prepare dressing, combine all ingredients and mix well.

This is a beautiful salad...so light and colorful.

SALADS

FRESH ASPARAGUS SALAD

1 head romaine lettuce,
  rinsed and torn into bite-
  size pieces
1 head red leaf lettuce,
  rinsed and torn into bite-
  size pieces
16 red pepper strips
8 yellow pepper strips
24 fresh asparagus spears,
  blanched and cooled
Pecans, toasted and
  cooled

DRESSING:
¼ cup vegetable oil
3 Tbsp. red wine vinegar
3 Tbsp. minced fresh
  parsley
1½ Tbsp. sugar
½ tsp. salt
½ tsp. garlic salt
¼ tsp. dried oregano
⅛ tsp. pepper

SERVES 8
Put lettuce on plate. Place two red pepper strips, one yellow pepper strip, and three asparagus spears on top of lettuce. Sprinkle with pecans. Pour dressing over top of salad and serve.

To make dressing, combine all ingredients in a jar. Cover and shake vigorously. Chill.

PAT'S CAULIFLOWER SALAD

1 head cauliflower,
  chopped in bite-sized
  pieces
1 red onion, diced
4 stalks celery, diced
1 cup sour cream
1 cup mayonnaise
1 tsp. dill weed
1½ tsp. seasoning salt
1 tsp. dried onion
1 tsp. parsley

SERVES 6-8
Combine cauliflower, onion, and celery. In a small bowl, combine sour cream, mayonnaise, and seasonings and mix well. Pour dressing over salad and toss to coat. Cover and refrigerate overnight to allow flavors to blend.

AVOCADO TOSSED SALAD

1 head lettuce, rinsed and
    torn into bite-sized
    pieces
2 tomatoes, chopped
½ cup sliced ripe olives
2 green onions, chopped
1 cup tortilla chips,
    crushed
½ cup shredded Cheddar
    cheese

DRESSING:
1 avocado, peeled and
    mashed
1 Tbsp. lemon juice
½ cup sour cream
⅓ cup vegetable oil
½ tsp. seasoning salt
½ tsp. sugar
¼ tsp. salt
¼ tsp. Tabasco
½ tsp. chili powder

SERVES 4

Combine salad ingredients, except tortilla chips. Toss with dressing. Add crushed chips just before serving.

To make dressing, combine ingredients and mix until thoroughly blended.

Men love this salad!

BEST BROCCOLI SALAD

3 cups broccoli florets
6 slices bacon, fried crisp,
    drained and crumbled
1 cup red onion, chopped
¾ cup Cheddar cheese,
    grated
½ cup raisins, (optional)

DRESSING:
1 cup mayonnaise
2 Tbsp. white vinegar
¼ cup sugar

SERVES 6

Toss together broccoli, bacon, onion, cheese, and raisins (if desired). Combine dressing ingredients and mix well. Pour over vegetables and toss to coat.

We love this salad because it is so different, goes well with beef or chicken, and is extra-easy to prepare.

SALADS

PATSY'S CABBAGE SALAD

1 — 3 oz. pkg. Oriental
  noodles, chicken flavor
4 cups shredded cabbage
4 green onions, chopped
2 Tbsp. sesame seeds

DRESSING:
Seasoning packet from
  noodles
3 Tbsp. vinegar
2 Tbsp. sugar
2 Tbsp. oil
½ tsp. pepper
¼ tsp. salt

½ cup slivered almonds,
  toasted

SERVES 6-8
Crush noodles slightly. Place in colander and pour boiling water over noodles to soften. Drain well. In a large bowl, combine noodles, cabbage, onions, and sesame seeds.

To make dressing, combine seasoning packet from noodles, vinegar, sugar, oil, pepper and salt in a jar. Shake well to mix.

Pour dressing over cabbage mixture and toss. Cover and chill several hours. Before serving, stir in almonds.

We love this salad when we go to Patsy's for a hamburger fry. It is great to take to a potluck or salad luncheon...so different and delicious!

CREAMY CAESAR SALAD

1 head Romaine lettuce
Croutons
Bacon bits
Parmesan cheese

DRESSING:
1 clove garlic, minced
1 egg
1 tsp. Worcestershire
  sauce
2 Tbsp. lemon juice
Dash pepper
1 cup olive oil

SERVES 6-8
Combine salad ingredients. Add chilled dressing just before serving and toss.

Combine first five dressing ingredients in a food processor or blender. Pour olive oil in a thin stream as the other ingredients are blending. Chill.

This wonderful salad is easy to make and goes well with most entrees. Tastes like you worked harder than you did!

SALADS

SOUTHERN SALAD

1 cucumber, peeled and
   sliced paper-thin
1 ripe tomato, sliced paper-
   thin
1 white onion, sliced
   paper-thin
1 tsp. sugar
Salt and freshly ground
   black pepper to taste
1 cup white vinegar

SERVES 6

Place vegetables in a bowl in layers, sprinkling sugar, salt and pepper on each layer. Cover with vinegar, using more if necessary. Let stand for 1 hour before serving to allow flavors to blend.

This traditional Southern-style salad is best if the vegetables are garden-fresh. You will be disappointed if you try this with store-bought cucumbers and tomatoes, so plan to make this a summertime taste treat for your family.

LETTUCE AND PEA SALAD

½ head romaine lettuce,
   torn
½ head iceberg lettuce,
   torn
2 stalks celery, sliced
   diagonally
2 green onions, sliced
1 cucumber, sliced
1 — 10 oz. pkg. frozen
   peas, thawed

DRESSING:
¼ cup vegetable oil
3 Tbsp. red wine vinegar
3 Tbsp. minced fresh
   parsley
1½ Tbsp. sugar
½ tsp. salt
½ tsp. garlic salt
¼ tsp. dried oregano
⅛ tsp. pepper

SERVES 4-6

Combine romaine lettuce and remaining ingredients in a zip-lock plastic bag. Chill at least 2 hours.

Combine dressing ingredients in a jar. Cover tightly and shake vigorously. Chill.

To serve, toss lettuce mixture with dressing, or divide lettuce evenly among salad plates and top with dressing.

SALADS

MANDARIN SALAD

Good! 8/08

SERVES 4-6

½ cup sliced almonds
3 Tbsp. sugar
½ head iceberg lettuce, torn into pieces
½ head romaine lettuce, torn into pieces
1 cup chopped celery
2 whole green onions, chopped
1 — 11 oz. can Mandarin oranges, drained

DRESSING:
½ tsp. salt
Dash of pepper
¼ cup vegetable oil
1 Tbsp. chopped parsley
2 Tbsp. sugar
2 Tbsp. vinegar
Dash of Tabasco

In a small pan over medium heat, cook almonds and sugar, stirring constantly until almonds are coated and sugar is dissolved. Watch carefully as they will burn easily. Cool and store in air-tight container. Mix lettuces, celery and onions. Just before serving add almonds and oranges. Toss with dressing.

To prepare dressing, mix ingredients in a screwtop jar and shake to blend. Chill.

2/11
Added chicken breast, water chestnuts, red pepper.
Very good
(used almond accents)
sm. amt Litehouse sesame ginger dressg.

ORANGE-ALMOND SALAD

SERVES 4

1 — 11 oz. can Mandarin oranges, drained (reserve juice)
2 Tbsp. reserved Mandarin juice
2 Tbsp. olive oil
1 Tbsp. cider vinegar
¼ tsp. salt
¼ tsp. black pepper
1 small head Romaine lettuce
¼ cup toasted slivered almonds

Drain Mandarin oranges, reserving 2 tablespoons juice. Mix juice, oil, vinegar, salt and pepper. Toss with oranges. Separate lettuce leaves and arrange on each plate. Spoon oranges on top lettuce and sprinkle with slivered almonds.

This light, tasty salad is wonderful with most any entree.

100

CRAZY MIXED-UP SALAD

1 — 31 - 17

1 — 16 oz. can red kidney
   beans, drained
1 — 16 oz. can garbanzo
   beans, drained
1 cup chopped celery
1 cup chopped cucumber
½ cup chopped green
   pepper
1 cup salsa
1 Tbsp. chopped cilantro
½ cup Italian dressing
1 avocado, peeled and
   chopped
1 tomato, chopped
4 slices bacon, cooked and
   crumbled

SERVES 6
Combine beans, celery, cucumber, green pepper, salsa, cilantro and Italian dressing. Stir gently to blend. Cover and refrigerate for at least 3 hours. Just before serving, stir in avocado, tomato, and bacon. Serve immediately.

This unusual salad is so good and easy. Goes well with hot sandwiches.

ORIENTAL SALAD

1 head leaf lettuce, torn
   into bite-sized pieces
4 green onions, sliced
3 oz. slivered almonds
4 tsp. sesame seeds
6-8 slices bacon, fried
   crisp and crumbled
½ cup Chinese noodles

DRESSING:
3 Tbsp. sugar
2 tsp. salt
2 tsp. Accent
¼ tsp. black pepper
½ cup vegetable oil
6 Tbsp. white vinegar

SERVES 6
Combine lettuce and onions. Toss with dressing and add remaining ingredients just before serving.

Combine all dressing ingredients and shake well to blend.

SALADS

PEA SALAD

1 cup dry roasted peanuts
1 cup chopped celery
1 small bunch green
   onions, chopped (about
   ½ cup)
4 slices bacon, fried and
   crumbled
1 — 10 oz. pkg. frozen peas
1 cup sour cream

SERVES 4
Combine peanuts, celery, green onions, and bacon. Just before serving
add peas and sour cream. Mix well
and serve on a bed of lettuce.

SALAD OF HEARTS

1 head red leaf lettuce
1 head Romaine lettuce
1 — 14 oz. can artichoke
   hearts
1 — 14 oz. can hearts of
   palm
2 medium tomatoes,
   chopped

MUSTARD VINAIGRETTE:
6 Tbsp. oil
2 Tbsp. fresh lemon juice
1 tsp. sugar
1 tsp. salt
1 tsp. freshly ground
   pepper
2 tsp. Dijon mustard
¼ tsp. garlic powder
1 tsp. Worcestershire
   sauce

SERVES 6
Tear chilled lettuce into bite-sized
pieces. Drain artichoke hearts and
quarter. Drain hearts of palm and
slice. Toss these ingredients with the
tomatoes in a large bowl. Add Mustard Vinaigrette and toss again.

To make vinaigrette, combine all ingredients in a jar with a lid. Shake to
blend and serve over salad.

SUPER SALAD

SALAD:
1 — 14 oz. can artichoke
   hearts, drained &
   quartered
2 cups fresh or frozen peas
1 large red onion, thinly
   sliced
½ lb. spinach leaves
1 head Bibb lettuce
1½ heads iceberg lettuce
2 ripe avocados, sliced
1 — 11 oz. can Mandarin
   oranges, drained
½ cup bleu cheese,
   crumbled (optional)

DRESSING:
¾ cup salad oil
¼ cup wine vinegar
½ tsp. salt
¼ tsp. sugar
¼ tsp. pepper

SERVES 4-6
Combine dressing ingredients in a medium saucepan. Bring to a boil, stirring occasionally. Cool.

In a large bowl, combine salad ingredients and toss well. Pour cooled dressing over salad and serve.

This is a really good salad that is easy to make, yet unusual enough to serve for a special occasion.

SALADS

SUSIE'S SALAD

1 — 8½ oz. can artichoke
   hearts, drained
1 — 10 oz. can hearts of
   palm, drained
1 head Romaine lettuce,
   torn into bite-sized
   pieces
1 head iceberg lettuce, torn
   into bite-sized pieces
1 — 4 oz. jar diced
   pimentos, drained
1 large red onion, thinly
   sliced
½ cup olive oil
⅓ cup tarragon vinegar
½ cup grated Parmesan
Salt and cracked pepper to
   taste

SERVES 6-8

Cut artichoke hearts into quarters. Slice hearts of palm. Toss in a salad bowl with lettuce, pimentos, and onions. Mix olive oil and vinegar. Pour over salad. Sprinkle with cheese, salt and pepper. Toss to serve.

This salad is great with lasagna or any Italian-style entree, though Susie often serves it with a grilled T-bone steak. Such a treat!

RASPBERRY SPINACH SALAD

8 cups fresh spinach,
   rinsed, stemmed and
   torn into pieces
½ cup sliced or slivered
   almonds
1 cup fresh raspberries
3 kiwis, peeled and sliced

DRESSING:
2 Tbsp. raspberry vinegar
2 Tbsp. seedless raspberry
   jam
⅓ cup vegetable oil

SERVES 8

In a flat salad bowl, toss the spinach, half of the almonds, raspberries, and kiwis with dressing. Top with remaining nuts and fruits. Serve immediately.

To make dressing, combine vinegar and jam in blender, food processor, or small bowl. Add oil in a thin stream, blending well until thickened.

This is a divine salad. It is easy and elegant and would do you proud at your next dinner party, salad luncheon, or as a special treat for your family!

EXCELLENT BEAN SALAD

1 cup each canned and
  drained:
  pinto beans
  black beans
  garbanzo beans
  cut green beans
  white beans
¼ cup chopped green
  pepper
1 cup thinly sliced red
  onion
1 medium tomato, chopped
½ cup mayonnaise

DRESSING:
2 Tbsp. cider vinegar
½ tsp. sugar
¼ tsp. salt
⅛ tsp. black pepper
½ tsp. Dijon mustard
5 Tbsp. olive oil

SERVES 6
In a large bowl, combine beans, bell pepper, and onion, taking care not to break beans.

Prepare dressing by mixing together all ingredients except the oil in a screwtop jar. Mix in olive oil and shake well.

Pour dressing over the salad and mix gently. Just before serving, stir in tomatoes and mayonnaise.

You can use as many different kinds of beans as you choose to personalize this salad.

ORANGE-BEET SALAD

2 oranges, sliced and
  peeled
1 — 8¼ oz. can sliced
  pickled beets
1 small purple onion, thinly
  sliced
Bibb lettuce leaves
½ cup creamy Italian
  dressing

SERVES 4
Arrange orange and beet slices on Bibb lettuce. Top with onion slice (or rings if you prefer). Pour dressing over top and serve.

SALADS

SPINACH WALDORF SALAD

4 cups fresh spinach, rinsed and torn into bite-size pieces
1 red apple, cored and cubed
1 yellow apple, cored and cubed
3 Tbsp. walnut pieces
3 Tbsp. raisins
Poppy Seed Dressing
Pinch of ground cinnamon

POPPY SEED DRESSING:
1¼ cups sugar
2 tsp. dry mustard
2 tsp. salt
⅔ cup vinegar
3 Tbsp. onion juice
2 cups salad oil (not olive oil)
3 Tbsp. poppy seeds

SERVES 6

Toss together the spinach, apple, walnuts and raisins. Pour about ¼ cup dressing over salad and toss well. (You can buy commercially prepared Poppy Seed Dressing, though homemade is better.) Sprinkle cinnamon over top of salad.

To make dressing, mix sugar, mustard, salt, and vinegar. Add onion juice and stir it in thoroughly. Add oil slowly, beating constantly until thick. Use a blender, food processor, or mixer for this part. Add poppy seeds, and beat until well blended.

This is a delightful variation of an old favorite...great way to get kids to eat spinach!

MARR-VELOUS SALAD

1-2 bunches fresh spinach
   leaves, torn into bite-
   sized pieces
1-2 pints fresh
   strawberries, sliced
   thickly
¼ cup sliced almonds

DRESSING:
3 Tbsp. sugar
1 tsp. dry mustard
1 tsp. salt
½ medium onion, chopped
½ cup salad oil
½ cup olive oil
⅓ cup red wine vinegar
2 Tbsp. poppy seeds

SERVES 6-8

In a large bowl, toss spinach, berries and almonds. Toss with dressing for a delightful summer salad.

To prepare dressing, combine everything but poppy seeds in a blender or food processor. Blend until thickened. Stir in poppy seeds. Makes 1 pint.

Very good ## TRICOLOR PASTA SALAD *1/08*

¼ cup olive oil
2 cups small broccoli
   florets
1 green bell pepper, diced
1 garlic clove, minced (or
   ¼ tsp. garlic powder)
½ tsp. dried basil
½ lb. tricolor fusilli pasta,
   cooked and cooled
1 cup cherry tomatoes,
   halved
⅓ cup sliced black olives
¼ cup olive oil ← *Used Canola*
2 Tbsp. red wine vinegar
1 cup grated Parmesan

SERVES 6-8

Heat ¼ cup oil in large skillet over medium-high heat. Add broccoli and next 4 ingredients and cook until broccoli is crisp-tender. Remove from heat. Toss with pasta. Mix in tomatoes and olives. Mix together olive oil and vinegar. Add to salad and toss well. Stir in Parmesan.

SALADS

MAIN DISH PASTA SALAD

1 —12 oz. pkg. tri-colored
  rotini noodles
12 oz. summer sausage
1 — 6 oz. jar marinated
  artichokes, cut in half
1 — 16 oz. can whole ripe
  olives, sliced
1 green pepper, cut in thin
  strips
1 red pepper, cut in thin
  strips
8 oz. cherry tomatoes, cut
  in half
1 bunch green onions,
  sliced
8 oz. fresh mushrooms,
  sliced
1 head broccoli, cut into
  small flowerettes
12 oz. Mozzarella, cubed
¼ cup Parmesan cheese,
  grated

DRESSING:
2 Tbsp. Dijon mustard
½ cup red wine vinegar
2 tsp. sugar
1 tsp. salt
1 tsp. black pepper
¼ cup fresh parsley,
  minced
1 Tbsp. fresh chives
½-1 tsp. oregano
½-1 tsp. thyme
1 cup olive oil

SERVES 15-20
Cook noodles according to package directions, drain. Cut sausage into thin slices, then strips. Mix noodles and sausage with other ingredients in a large bowl. Toss with dressing. Chill before serving.

To prepare dressing measure mustard in a bowl. Whisk in vinegar, sugar, salt, pepper and herbs. Continue to whisk mixture while slowly dribbling in olive oil until mixture thickens. Adjust seasonings to taste.

You will love this salad for potlucks, salad luncheons, or family reunions.

PASTA PERFECTION

1 lb. rotini or shell
   macaroni
½ cucumber
½ large green pepper
1 bunch green onions
4 hard-cooked eggs
1 small jar pimentos
1 bunch radishes
1½ tsp. salt
¾ tsp. pepper
1 tsp. sugar
½ tsp. celery seed
½ tsp. leaf oregano

DRESSING:
2 cups mayonnaise
¾ cup sour cream
¾ cup half and half or milk
4 Tbsp. honey mustard
1 Tbsp. yellow mustard

SERVES 8-10
Boil macaroni; drain and cool. Chop cucumber, pepper, green onions, eggs, pimentos, and slice radishes very thin. Mix thoroughly in large bowl. Add pasta to vegetables. Add seasonings, then stir in dressing, mixing well.

To prepare dressing, mix all ingredients until thoroughly blended. If it is too thick, add more milk or cream.

SALADS

MOLDED CHICKEN SALAD

1 envelope unflavored
  gelatin
1 cup cold water
1 cup chicken stock,
  heated to boiling
1 cup toasted, slivered
  almonds
4 cups cubed cooked
  chicken
4 hard-cooked eggs,
  chopped
1 cup celery, finely
  chopped
1 — 7½ oz. can green peas,
  drained
2 cups mayonnaise
Cayenne pepper

SERVES 12

In a large bowl, soften gelatin in cold water. Add boiling chicken stock and stir to dissolve. Add nuts, chicken, eggs, celery, peas, mayonnaise. Sprinkle with cayenne and stir. Pour into a 9 x 13 inch glass dish and chill until firm. Cut into squares to serve.

Good with fresh fruit and croissants for a summer luncheon.

WILD RICE CHICKEN SALAD

⅔ cup mayonnaise
⅓ cup milk
2 Tbsp. lemon juice
¼ tsp. summer savory
3 cups cooked cubed
  chicken
3 cups cooked wild rice
⅓ cup finely chopped
  green onion
1 — 8 oz. can sliced water
  chestnuts, drained
½ tsp. salt
⅛ tsp. pepper
1 cup seedless green
  grapes, halved
1 cup salted cashews,
  chopped

SERVES 6

Blend mayonnaise, milk, lemon juice and summer savory. Set aside. In large bowl, combine chicken, wild rice, onion, water chestnuts, salt and pepper. Stir in mayonnaise mixture until blended. Refrigerate, covered, 2 to 3 hours. Just before serving, fold in grapes and cashews.

CHICKEN IN A CREAM PUFF

CHICKEN SALAD:
2 cups cubed, cooked
  chicken
1 cup seedless green
  grapes, halved
½ cup shredded Swiss
  cheese
½ cup sliced celery
3 Tbsp. sliced green
  onions
½ cup dairy sour cream
¼ cup mayonnaise
¼ cup cashews or toasted
  sliced almonds
Salt to taste

CREAM PUFF:
¼ cup margarine
1 cup boiling water
1 cup flour
¼ tsp. salt
4 eggs

Leaf lettuce, garnish

SERVES 4-6
Combine chicken, grapes, cheese, celery, onion, sour cream and mayonnaise. Chill until ready to serve.

To make cream puff, add margarine to boiling water and stir until melted; add flour and salt all at once. Stir until well blended and a ball forms. Set aside to cool for 10 minutes. Add eggs to flour mixture, one at a time. Stir after each addition until thoroughly blended. Butter a 9-inch pie pan. Spread batter evenly in bottom and on side. Bake at 400° for 30-35 minutes or until puffed and lightly browned.

When ready to serve, line pastry with lettuce leaves and fill with chicken salad. Sprinkle chopped nuts on top. Cut into wedges to serve.

SALADS

CRABACADO SALAD

2 cups crabmeat (frozen, canned or fresh)
½ cup sliced green onions
⅓ cup canned Mandarin orange sections, drained
5 Tbsp. vegetable oil
2½ Tbsp. white wine vinegar
½ tsp. garlic salt
Pepper
2 avocados, halved and pitted

SERVES 4

Mix together first six ingredients. Season with pepper. Spoon over avocado halves. Serve immediately.

This makes a nice luncheon dish.

MARINATED SHRIMP SALAD

2½ lbs. shrimp, cooked
2 cups sliced white onions (try Vidalia onions, they are so sweet and mild)
Bay leaves

MARINADE:
1¼ cups vegetable oil
¾ cup white vinegar
2½ tsp. celery seed
½ tsp. coarsely ground pepper
1 dash Worcestershire sauce
1 dash Tabasco sauce

Bibb lettuce leaves

SERVES 8

Alternate shrimp and onions in a shallow dish. Add bay leaves. Combine marinade ingredients and pour over shrimp. Cover and refrigerate for at least 24 hours.

Arrange Bibb lettuce on each plate. Remove bay leaves from shrimp mixture, and arrange shrimp and onions on lettuce. Sprinkle marinade as a dressing on top of this.

This is a superb salad…would be a good appetizer, too.

SNAPPY SHRIMP SALAD

1 medium red onion
1 red bell pepper
1 green bell pepper
3 medium tomatoes
1½ lbs. medium raw
  shrimp, shelled and
  deveined
½ cup ripe black olives,
  halved
½ cup stuffed green olives,
  halved

JALAPENO DRESSING:
½ tsp. garlic powder
1-2 Tbsp. diced, canned
  jalapeno chilies
½ cup olive oil
⅓ cup lemon juice
1 tsp. ground cumin
1 bay leaf
½ tsp. salt
Pepper

SERVES 6-8
Slice the onion, red and green peppers and tomatoes into julienne strips. Place the shrimp in boiling water and cook just until they turn pink, about 2 minutes. Combine all the ingredients in a serving bowl, and toss with the dressing.

To prepare dressing, combine all ingredients in a screwtop jar and shake to blend. Remove bay leaf before using.

COACH KELLEY'S FIRST PLACE SHRIMP SALAD

8 oz. pasta, cooked and
  drained
1 lb. crab, chopped (frozen
  or canned)
1 lb. cooked shrimp
½ cup diced onion
½ cup diced green pepper
1½ cups diced celery
⅛ tsp. garlic salt
1 cup Miracle Whip
2 Tbsp. wine vinegar
Salt and pepper to taste

SERVES 4-6
Combine pasta with crab, shrimp, onion, green pepper, and celery. In a small bowl, mix together the garlic salt, Miracle Whip, vinegar, salt and pepper. Blend into pasta/shrimp mixture. Refrigerate to blend flavors.

This one is a real winner!

SALADS

STEAK SALAD

¼ cup red wine vinegar
¼ cup olive oil
1 clove garlic, minced
1 jar marinated artichoke
   hearts, sliced, with
   liquid
1 tsp. sugar
1 tsp. salt
½ tsp. black pepper
½ tsp. oregano
½ tsp. rosemary
2 lbs. boneless T-bone
   steak, 1-inch thick,
   broiled and sliced paper
   thin
1 large red onion, thinly
   sliced
1 dozen cherry tomatoes
1 cup fresh mushrooms,
   sliced
5 cups fresh spinach,
   washed and drained

SERVES 6
Whisk vinegar into olive oil. Add garlic, liquid from artichoke hearts, sugar, salt, pepper and herbs. Add steak, onion, tomatoes, and mushrooms. Marinate one hour. Arrange spinach in bowl. Add marinated ingredients and artichoke hearts and toss. Spoon marinade over salad and serve at once.

MEATS

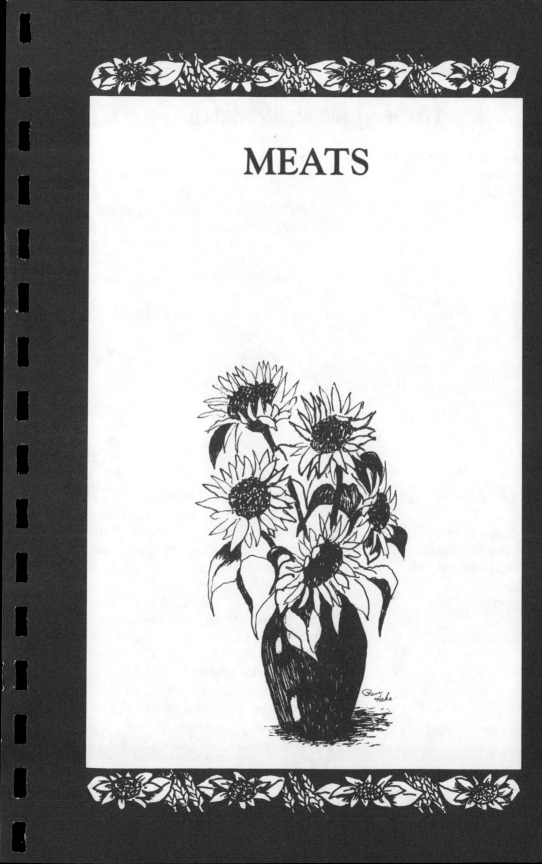

MEATS

THE BEST BEEF TENDERLOIN

1 — 2-3 lb. beef tenderloin
Lemon pepper
1 Tbsp. oil

SERVES 4

Season both sides of tenderloin liberally with lemon pepper. Heat oil in a cast iron skillet, and brown tenderloin over medium high heat, turning it over and over. Place tenderloin in a shallow baking dish, and bake at 350° for 30 minutes for medium rare. Slice to serve.

This is the best beef recipe ever. Though tenderloin is expensive, it is low in fat and absolutely delicious when prepared this way.

PRIME RIB

1 boneless rib roast, any
    size
1 large onion, sliced
⅓ cup vermouth
⅓ cup cooking oil
Salt
Pepper

2 SERVINGS PER POUND

Preheat oven to 500°. Lay onion slices in the bottom of an open roasting pan. Place prime rib in pan. Mix vermouth and cooking oil and pour over roast. Season liberally with salt and pepper. Cook roast 5 minutes per pound. When meat has cooked the allotted time, turn off the oven. DO NOT OPEN OVEN DOOR. Let meat rest for at least 1 hour and up to 2. When ready to serve, remove from oven and slice. Meat will be rare and juicy. For medium-rare, add 5 minutes to total cooking time. For medium, add 10 minutes.

CHUCK ROAST WITH MUSHROOMS

5-6 lb. chuck roast
2 — 2½ oz. can button
  mushrooms

MARINADE:
¼ cup olive oil
¼ cup vegetable oil
1 tsp. dried parsley
1 Tbsp. salt
1 tsp. pepper
2 Tbsp. honey
½ tsp. dry mustard
½ tsp. soy sauce
Dash Tabasco sauce
1 Tbsp. lemon juice
2 Tbsp. steak sauce
¼ cup wine vinegar
¼ cup cooking sherry
4 Tbsp. ketchup

SERVES 4-6

Combine marinade ingredients in a saucepan and heat thoroughly. Place meat in a glass baking dish and pour heated marinade over it. Pierce meat with a fork to allow marinade to soak in. Cover with plastic wrap and refrigerate at least 3 hours. Turn meat several times.

Pour off marinade and save it. Place meat in a roaster pan and bake covered at 350° for 2½ to 3 hours. Baste occasionally.

Before serving, heat reserved marinade in saucepan. Add mushrooms and cook for 5 minutes or until heated. Place mushrooms on and around roast before serving. Pass marinade as gravy for roast.

This variation on a plain chuck roast is a welcome treat.

SUNDAY DINNER

1 — 3½ lb. boneless chuck
  roast
1 — 10 oz. can cream of
  celery soup
½ pkg. dry onion soup mix
4 potatoes, peeled
6 carrots, peeled
8 celery stalks
¼ lb. fresh mushrooms,
  sliced
½ cup red wine

SERVES 4

Place roast in a large baking pan. Spread celery soup on top and sprinkle onion soup over all. Cut potatoes in half and carrots in chunks. Add to roast. Cover and bake at 300° for 2 hours. Cut celery in 1 inch chunks and add with mushrooms. Add wine and spoon sauce over all. Bake for 1 hour longer, or until roast is fork-tender.

MEATS

WILMA'S FLAVORFUL POT ROAST

3-4 lb. chuck roast
2 cups water
1 envelope onion soup mix
Salt
Pepper

SERVES 6

Set pot roast in roasting pan, sprinkle liberally with salt and pepper. Stir onion soup mix into water and add to roast. Cover and cook at 275° for about 4 hours, or until meat is fork-tender.

This is a delicious version of an old stand-by!

RO-TEL ROAST

1 — 4 lb. chuck roast
2 — 10 oz. cans Ro-Tel tomatoes (tomatoes with green chilies)
Salt and pepper

SERVES 4-6

Season roast with salt and pepper. Pour Ro-Tel tomatoes over roast. Cover and bake at 275° for 3-4 hours.

BEER BRISKET

1 — 16 oz. jar picante sauce
1 — 12 oz. can beer
1 pkg. dry onion soup mix
4-6 lb. beef brisket

SERVES 6

Mix together the first three ingredients and pour over brisket. Cover and bake at 250° for 6 hours, or until beef is fork-tender. Uncover the last ½ hour.

STROGANOFF STEAK SANDWICH

⅔ cup beer
⅓ cup vegetable oil
1 tsp. salt
¼ tsp. garlic powder
¼ tsp. coarse pepper
2 to 2½ lbs. flank steak
2 Tbsp. butter
½ tsp. paprika
4 cups sliced onions
1 — 12 oz. carton sour
  cream
½ to 1 tsp. horseradish
12 slices French bread

SERVES 6

Combine beer, oil, salt, garlic, and pepper. Place flank steak in marinade; cover and refrigerate overnight. Turn occasionally. Drain and barbecue or broil 5-7 minutes on each side for medium rare. In a saucepan, melt butter and paprika. Add a dash of salt, cook onions until just tender. In another saucepan, warm sour cream and horseradish. Toast French bread just lightly. Slice meat very thinly across the grain. Place meat over toast, cover with onions and then sour cream. Sprinkle with paprika.

Great Sunday afternoon meal...goes with football and beer!

CARNE ASADA

1 cup oil
½ cup lemon juice
2 tsp. paprika
4 Tbsp. Worcestershire
  sauce
Dash Tabasco sauce
4 Tbsp. vinegar
2 Tbsp. salt
4 Tbsp. sugar
1 tsp. garlic powder
1-2 lb. flank steak

SERVES 4

Mix marinade ingredients together. Place flank steak in a 9 x 13 inch dish and pour marinade over. Cover and refrigerate overnight, turning occasionally. Grill meat over hot coals to desired doneness. Slice thinly to serve. Also a good marinade for shish-ka-bob meat.

You can't beat this for an easy main dish for your next backyard barbecue.

MEATS

PONY EXPRESS STEAK

1½ lbs. boneless beef top
   sirloin steak, cut 1-inch
   thick
¼ tsp. pepper
1 tsp. garlic powder
1 tsp. butter
2 tsp. vegetable oil
¾ tsp. salt
1 red bell pepper, thinly
   sliced
1 green bell pepper, thinly
   sliced
1 small onion, thinly sliced
1 cup sliced mushrooms
⅓ cup walnuts, chopped
¼ tsp. chili powder
1 Tbsp. sour cream
1 — 4 oz. can diced green
   chilies, drained

SERVES 6

Lightly pound steak to about ¼ inch thickness. Sprinkle with pepper and ½ tsp. garlic powder. Heat 1 tsp. oil and butter in large skillet until hot. Sprinkle with ½ teaspoon salt. Add steak, frying about 3 minutes on each side. Remove steak to 9 x 13 inch baking dish and keep warm. Add remaining vegetable oil to drippings and saute vegetables and walnuts about 2 minutes blending well. Add remaining garlic powder, salt, and chili powder. Saute 2 more minutes. Remove from heat and cover.

Spread sour cream and diced chilies on top of steak. Layer vegetables on top of chilies. Cover and bake at 350° until heated through.

STEAK FINGERS

Tenderized round steak
Flour
Cracker crumbs
Beaten eggs
Oil for frying

Cut meat in ½-inch slices. Mix flour and cracker crumbs (half and half). Beat eggs with a little water. Dip meat strips in flour mixture, then egg mixture, then flour mixture again. Fry in hot shortening until done.

Serve with cocktail sauce, sour cream/ horseradish mixture, or a cream gravy for dipping. Use proportions to fit your family.

FAVORITE PEPPER STEAK

1½ lbs. top sirloin, 1-inch
  thick
¼ cup vegetable oil
¼ tsp. garlic powder
1 tsp. ginger
1 tsp. salt
¼ tsp. pepper
2 green peppers, sliced
2 large onions, thinly
  sliced
¼ cup soy sauce
½ tsp. sugar
1 cup beef bouillon
1 — 8 oz. can water
  chestnuts, sliced
4 green onions, chopped
2 Tbsp. cornstarch
¼ cup cold water
2 firm tomatoes, peeled
  and cut into eighths
Hot cooked rice

SERVES 4-6

Cut meat into ⅛ inch slices. (This works better if the meat is slightly frozen.) Heat oil in skillet and add garlic powder, salt, ginger and pepper. Saute about a minute. Add steak slices and brown lightly. Remove meat. Add green pepper and onion. Cook 7-10 minutes. Return beef to pan. Add soy sauce, sugar, bouillon, water chestnuts, green onions, and cornstarch dissolved in water. Simmer 3 minutes or until sauce thickens. Add tomatoes and heat. Serve over hot rice. Top with extra soy sauce if desired.

So tasty!

PAUL'S COUNTRY FRIED STEAK

2 to 2½ lbs. boneless round steak, tenderized and cut into serving size pieces
1 tsp. salt
¼ tsp. pepper
1 cup flour
½ cup bacon drippings
1 medium onion, chopped
2 Tbsp. flour
1-2 cups water or milk
1 — 6 oz. can sliced mushrooms

SERVES 6-8

Combine flour, salt and pepper in a plastic bag. Drop pieces of steak into bag and shake to coat well. Heat bacon drippings in an iron skillet until hot. Brown steak in drippings, remove from pan, drain, and transfer to a 9 x 13 inch baking pan.

Add chopped onions to skillet and saute until tender. Add 2 Tbsp. flour and brown until darkened. Add 1-2 cups water or milk gradually to browned flour to make a gravy, stirring as it thickens. Add mushrooms.

Pour gravy over steak, cover, and bake at 325° 30-45 minutes until tender. If gravy begins to thicken too much, add some water or milk.

Paul is our resident expert on country fried steak...his version is most delicious!

EASY BEEF TIPS

2 lbs. lean chuck, cubed
1 — 10 oz. can cream of mushroom soup
1 envelope dry onion soup mix
1 cup 7-Up

SERVES 4

Place meat in a 2 quart casserole. Do not season. Pour soup and soup mix over meat. Add 7-Up. Cover and bake at 275° for 4 hours. Do NOT open oven door during cooking. Let stand 30 minutes before serving. Great over mashed potatoes, this easy beef dish makes it own gravy and has a wonderful flavor.

ROUND STEAK SAUERBRATEN

1½ lb. round steak
1 Tbsp. bacon drippings
1 envelope brown gravy
   mix
2 cups water
1 Tbsp. instant minced
   onion
2 Tbsp. white wine vinegar
2 Tbsp. brown sugar
½ tsp. salt
1 tsp. Worcestershire
   sauce
1 bay leaf
Hot buttered noodles

SERVES 4-6

Cut meat into 1-inch squares. In large skillet, brown meat on all sides in hot drippings. Remove meat from skillet; add gravy mix and water. Bring to boil, stirring constantly. Stir in remaining ingredients except noodles. Return meat to skillet; cover and simmer 1½ hours, stirring occasionally. Remove bay leaf. Serve meat over hot buttered noodles.

SWISS FAMILY STEAK

3 Tbsp. flour
¼ tsp. salt
¼ tsp. pepper
1½ lbs. cubed steak, cut
   into strips
4 Tbsp. vegetable oil
1 onion, chopped
1 large celery stalk, sliced
1 large carrot, thinly sliced
¼ tsp. garlic powder
1 — 14½ oz. can stewed
   tomatoes
½ cup red cooking wine
1 tsp. dried oregano
1 tsp. dried savory
Salt and pepper to taste

SERVES 4

Combine flour, salt, pepper in a zip-lock bag. Shake steak pieces in flour mixture. Reserve remaining flour. Heat oil in a skillet over high heat. Brown steak pieces (about 2 minutes per side) and transfer to 9 x 13 inch baking dish.

Reduce heat and add vegetables. Saute about 5 minutes. Add garlic and reserved flour and cook to thicken, stirring constantly. Add stewed tomatoes, wine, oregano and savory. Add salt and pepper to taste. Cover and bake at 350° for 30 minutes.

Serve with mashed potatoes and green beans for a hearty dinner.

MEATS

RANCHER'S BEEF RIBS

5 lbs. beef short ribs
3 cups cola
2 Tbsp. lemon juice
2 tsp. garlic powder
1½ tsp. coarsely ground
  pepper
½ cup vegetable oil
1 cup ketchup
1 Tbsp. instant beef
  bouillon granules
2 Tbsp. prepared mustard
Salt

SERVES 8

Combine cola, lemon juice, garlic and onion powders, and pepper. Arrange ribs in a single layer in a 9 x 13 inch baking dish. Pour cola mixture over ribs; marinate 30-45 minutes. Drain ribs, reserving marinade. Heat oil in roasting pan in 375° oven until sizzling. Add ribs; brown in oven about 30-45 minutes, turning once or until ribs are rich caramel color. Pour off drippings.

Combine ketchup, beef granules and mustard. Stir into reserved marinade; pour over ribs. Cover pan and bake at 300° for 2 to 2½ hours or until tender. Remove ribs to serving platter. Spoon fat from pan juices. Add salt to taste and serve ribs with pan juices.

MEATS

WEDDING BEEF

4 lbs. beef cubes (chuck or round steak)
1 large onion
Salt and pepper to taste

SERVES 6-8

Put beef in a roaster pan or Dutch oven. Add onion, chopped if you prefer, or whole just for the flavor. Salt and pepper to taste. Do not add water. Cover and cook at 275° for about 4 hours. Check every now and then, making sure the beef is not cooking dry. If so, add a little water, but usually this recipe requires nothing more than a little time.

Wedding Beef is historically called Threshers Meat as it was typically served to the large threshing crews at harvesting time. Recently, it has become a favorite dish to serve at wedding dinners in our area. The larger the batch, the better it tastes. It does make a wonderful banquet main dish and is especially good with mashed potatoes, green beans, salad and homemade rolls.

MEATS

CHILI SUPREME

1 lb. stew meat
¼ tsp. paprika
½ tsp. cumin
1 Tbsp. chili powder
¼ tsp. garlic powder
¼-½ tsp. cayenne pepper
1 tsp. salt
¼ tsp. pepper
2 Tbsp. diced jalapenos
2-3 Tbsp. flour
¼ cup water
2 cups uncooked macaroni
½ cup Cheddar cheese,
   shredded
4 eggs, fried

SERVES 4

Cover meat with water. Cook until meat completely breaks apart. Add spices and simmer 30 minutes. Whisk together the flour and water. Stir into chili to thicken. Cook macaroni in boiling salted water until softened. Drain.

To serve, spoon a portion of macaroni into each individual bowl. Ladle chili on top to cover. Sprinkle with Cheddar cheese. Top with a fried egg.

This is another easy, filling meal. Serve with crackers or cornbread and a tossed green salad. Would be great to serve after a cold day on the slopes!

ENCHILADA CASSEROLE

2 lbs. ground beef
1 medium onion, chopped
1 lb. Velveeta cheese,
   chunked
1 — 10½ oz. can cream of
   mushroom soup
1 — 10½ oz. can cream of
   chicken soup
1 — 10½ oz. can mild, red
   enchilada sauce
1 — 4 oz. can chopped
   green chilies
12 corn tortillas, quartered

SERVES 6

Brown ground beef and onion in a large skillet. Drain grease. Stir in Velveeta, soups, enchilada sauce, and green chilies until well blended. Spoon some of the meat mixture in the bottom of a 2½ quart casserole. Then put a layer of tortillas, then more meat. Continue layering ending with meat. Bake, covered, at 350° for 45 minutes to 1 hour. Freezes well.

Men love this casserole. Serve with a pot of beans and a tossed salad for a great meal.

PITA FAJITAS

4 lb. beef chuck roast
**1 — 7 oz. can diced green
  chilies**
3 Tbsp. chili powder
1 tsp. dried oregano
½ tsp. garlic powder
**1 — 8 oz. can stewed
  tomatoes**
Salt
Cayenne pepper
8 whole pita breads

Guacamole
Sour cream
Salsa

SERVES 8

Place roast on a large sheet of aluminum foil. Mix together green chilies, chili powder, oregano and garlic. Spread mixture on top of roast. Wrap foil around roast and seal. Place in a roaster pan and bake at 300° for 4-4½ hours or until meat falls off the bone. Unwrap roast and bone meat. Shred meat and add to pan drippings. Stir in tomatoes and heat through. Season with salt and cayenne to taste. Cut pita breads in half. Fill with beef mixture and garnish with guacamole, sour cream, and salsa.

Don't limit yourself to filling pita halves with this tasty beef...try it in tacos, burritos or just by itself!

MEATS

CHALUPAS DE LA CASA

6 corn tortillas
1 cup cooking oil
½ lb. ground beef
½ tsp. cumin
¼ tsp. chili powder
1 tsp. salt
1½ cups bean dip
2 cups grated Monterey
  Jack or Cheddar cheese

GARNISHES:
6 tsp. finely chopped green
  onion
¾ cup chopped tomatoes
3 cups finely chopped
  lettuce
¾ cup guacamole
6 Tbsp. sour cream

SERVES 4-6

Heat oil in a 10-inch skillet. Fry each tortilla in hot oil until crisp. Drain on paper towels and set aside. Remove remaining oil, and brown ground beef in same skillet. Add cumin, chili powder and salt. Remove from heat. Spread each tortilla with ¼ cup bean dip. Layer about 2 Tbsp. meat mixture on top. Sprinkle ⅓ cup cheese over meat. Place on a cookie sheet and bake at 350° until heated through.

While hot, place on individual plates and garnish each with onion, tomatoes, lettuce, guacamole and sour cream. Serve immediately.

COMPANY RELLENOS

TOMATO SAUCE:
1 — 1 lb. can stewed
   tomatoes
½ cup tomato juice
3 Tbsp. chili mix
   (preferably Williams
   brand)
1 tsp. cumin
1 tsp. sugar

RELLENOS:
5 — 4 oz. cans whole green
   chilies
1 lb. ground beef
1 onion, chopped
½ tsp. garlic powder
3 Tbsp. chili mix (Williams
   if you can find it)
1 tsp. cumin
½ tsp. salt
8 oz. Monterey Jack
   cheese, grated
8 oz. Cheddar cheese,
   grated
1 — 13 oz. can evaporated
   milk
4 eggs, beaten
1 Tbsp. flour

GARNISH:
Sour cream, raisins, pecan
   pieces

SERVES 8-10
Start tomato sauce first by mixing all ingredients together in a saucepan and simmering about 30 minutes or until slightly thickened.

To make casserole, rinse chilies, open out and remove seeds. Drain on paper towels. Brown ground beef and onions in a large skillet. Add seasonings and mix well. In a greased 9 x 13 inch casserole, make a single layer of chilies, using half. Add ground beef mixture and top with other half of chilies. Sprinkle with mixture of cheeses. In a bowl, add evaporated milk to eggs. Add flour, beating until well mixed. Pour egg mixture over cheeses.

Lightly cover top of casserole with prepared tomato sauce. If casserole is made early in the day, it is best to wait and put sauce on just before baking. Bake at 350° for 30-45 minutes. Edges should be browned and middle looking set and firm. To serve, cut in squares and top each with a dollop of sour cream. Sprinkle with raisins and pecan pieces. Serve with guacamole salad for an outstanding meal!

This casserole can be made ahead and frozen. Cook before freezing, and reheat at 300° uncovered.

MEATS

ENCHILADA STACK-UP

1½ lbs. ground beef
1 small onion, chopped
1 — 8 oz. can tomato sauce
1 — 4 oz. can chopped
   green chilies
1½ tsp. chili powder
½ tsp. salt
⅛ tsp. pepper
1 — 16 oz. can pinto beans
Dash Tabasco sauce
1 cup Cheddar cheese,
   grated
1 bag tortilla chips
1 cup tomato juice

GARNISH:
Sour cream
Chopped lettuce
Chopped tomatoes
Picante sauce
Chopped olives

SERVES 6
Brown ground beef and onion. Drain. Add tomato sauce, green chilies, chili powder, salt, pepper, beans, and Tabasco. Stir well.

In a 2 quart casserole, layer ¼ meat mixture, tortilla chips, and Cheddar cheese. Continue layering these ingredients making 4 layers. Pour 1 cup tomato juice around edge of stack. Cover and cook at 325° for 1 hour.

Can also be made in a slow cooker. Cover and cook on low for 4 hours or on high for 2 hours.

CHILE RELLENOS

12 fresh Anaheim green chilies
1 pound Monterey Jack cheese, cut into 12 even strips
¼ cup chopped onion
Oil for frying

BATTER:
½ cup flour
½ tsp. baking soda
½ tsp. salt
2 Tbsp. flat beer
2 eggs, separated
1-2 Tbsp. water

SERVES 6-8

Place chilies on a baking sheet; broil 5-6 inches from heat, turning often with tongs, until chilies are blistered on all sides. Immediately place in a zip-lock bag and fasten. Let steam 10-15 minutes. Remove peel of each chile, leaving stems intact. Cut a small slit below the stem of each pepper and carefully remove seeds. Stuff each chile with 1 piece of cheese and 1 teaspoon onion. The chilies will tear easily, so work carefully. Secure with toothpicks and set aside.

To prepare batter, blend together dry ingredients. Beat together beer and egg yolks. Combine with dry ingredients. Add only enough water to make a light batter the consistency of pancake batter. Beat egg whites until stiff. Fold into batter. Dip stuffed chilies into batter.

Pour oil to a depth of 2 inches into a skillet; heat to 375°. Fry chilies turning once, until golden brown. Serve immediately.

These are a special treat, well worth the effort involved in making them.

MEATS

SOUTHWESTERN SURPRISE

BATTER:
½ cup bacon drippings
1 cup yellow cornmeal
2 eggs, well-beaten
1 — 14 oz. can sweetened,
   condensed milk (not
   evaporated)
½ tsp. baking soda
1 tsp. salt
1 — 16 oz. can cream-style
   corn

FILLING:
½ lb. ground beef
½ lb. sausage
½ green pepper, chopped
1 medium onion, chopped
2 cups Longhorn cheese,
   grated
1 or 2 Tbsp. chopped
   jalapeno peppers (to
   taste)

SERVES 6-8

Mix batter ingredients and set aside. Brown beef, sausage, green pepper, and onion. Drain well.

Pour ½ batter into a well-greased 9 x 13 inch pan. Add meat mixture, then cheese. Sprinkle jalapeno peppers on top of the cheese. Pour remaining batter on top. Bake 25-35 minutes at 350° (or until center doesn't wiggle when you shake the pan.) Cut in squares and serve.

COWPUNCHER'S STEW

6 slices bacon, cooked and crumbled
1 medium onion, chopped
½ cup green pepper, chopped (optional)
¼ tsp. garlic powder
1½ lbs. ground beef
1 — 10 oz. can Ro-Tel tomatoes
2 — 14 oz. cans chopped tomatoes
1 — 12 oz. can corn
1 — 16 oz. can pinto beans (or red kidney beans, whatever you like)
3 medium potatoes, peeled and chopped
1 Tbsp. chili powder
Salt and pepper to taste
Grated Cheddar cheese

SERVES 6

Saute onion and green pepper in bacon drippings. Add garlic powder and ground beef and cook until browned. Drain. Add tomatoes, corn, beans, potatoes, and seasonings. Simmer 30 minutes. Serve with sprinkled bacon and/or cheese on each bowlful.

This stew is so easy and especially filling. Can be made in one pan so would be great after a busy day at work. Makes a delicious one-pot campfire meal as well!

MEATS

ZESTY MEATBALLS AND PEPPERS

MEATBALLS:
1½ lb. ground beef
½ cup finely chopped
   onion
⅓ cup dry bread crumbs
¼ tsp. garlic powder
¼ tsp. salt
⅛ tsp. pepper
1 egg, slightly beaten

SAUCE:
½ cup grape jelly
2 Tbsp. vinegar
1 — 12 oz. bottle chili
   sauce
1 medium green pepper,
   chopped
1 medium red bell pepper,
   chopped
1 medium yellow bell
   pepper, chopped

MAKES 30 MEATBALLS
In a large bowl, combine all meatball ingredients; blend well. Shape into 1-inch balls. Cook carefully in a skillet. Drain.

In a large saucepan, combine grape jelly, vinegar and chili sauce. Bring to a boil over medium heat. Reduce heat and simmer 5 minutes, stirring occasionally. Add meatballs and peppers; stir to coat. Cook over medium heat about 5 more minutes or until heated through.

UPSIDE DOWN PIZZA CASSEROLE

1 lb. ground beef
1 cup chopped onions
1 — 2 oz. can sliced black
  olives, drained
1 — 15 oz. can pizza sauce
¼ lb. pepperoni, coarsely
  chopped
½ tsp. dried Italian
  seasoning
1 — 4 oz. can sliced
  mushrooms, drained
6 oz. thinly sliced
  Mozzarella cheese

TOPPING:
1 cup milk
1 Tbsp. oil
2 eggs
1 cup flour
¼ tsp. salt
¼ cup Parmesan cheese

SERVES 6-8

In a large skillet over medium-high heat, brown ground beef and onions. Drain. Stir in olives, pizza sauce, pepperoni, seasoning, and mushrooms. Bring to a boil. Reduce heat to low; simmer uncovered 10 minutes, stirring occasionally.

Meanwhile in a small bowl, combine milk, oil and eggs; beat 1 minute at medium speed. Add flour and salt; beat 2 minutes at medium speed or until smooth. Spoon meat mixture evenly into ungreased 9 x 13 inch dish. Place cheese slices over hot meat mixture. Pour topping evenly over cheese, covering completely; sprinkle with Parmesan. Bake at 400° for 20-30 minutes or until puffed and deep golden.

MEATS

MOZZARELLA MEATBALLS

SAUCE:
2 — 28 oz. cans Italian
  tomatoes
1 tsp. garlic powder
1½ tsp. dried basil
1½ tsp. dried parsley
Salt and pepper to taste

MEATBALLS:
2 lbs. ground beef
6 saltine crackers, crushed
¼ cup water
⅓ cup grated Romano
  cheese
1 tsp. garlic powder
1½ tsp. dried parsley
½ tsp. salt
¼ tsp. pepper
½ lb. Mozzarella cheese,
  cubed
2-3 Tbsp. vegetable oil

1 lb. linguini or spaghetti
Romano cheese

SERVES 6

Drain tomatoes, reserving liquid. Crush tomatoes finely with a fork or in a food processor. In a saucepan, combine tomato liquid, garlic powder, basil, and parsley. Bring to a boil; reduce heat to low. Add crushed tomatoes; simmer uncovered 30 minutes stirring occasionally. Add salt and pepper if desired.

Combine ground beef, crackers, water, ⅓ cup cheese, garlic powder, parsley, salt and pepper, mixing lightly but thoroughly. Shape into 2-inch meatballs around a cube of Mozzarella cheese. Brown meatballs in oil in skillet. Drain. Add sauce and simmer uncovered 30 minutes. Meanwhile, cook linguini according to package directions; drain well. Serve meatballs and sauce over hot cooked pasta. Sprinkle with remaining cheese.

136

PIZZA PUFFS

1 — 12 oz. tube refrigerator
   biscuits
½ lb. ground beef
½ lb. Italian sausage
½ onion, chopped
1 — 16 oz. jar pizza sauce
1 cup grated Mozzarella
   cheese

MAKES 10

Grease 10 cups in a 12-cup muffin tin. Split biscuits and pat into bottom and sides of greased muffin tin. Brown ground beef, sausage, and onion in a skillet. Drain grease. Stir in pizza sauce and heat through. Place a spoonful of pizza mixture in each biscuit cup. Top with Mozzarella cheese. Bake at 400° to 8-10 minutes. Remove from muffin cups to plates to serve.

So easy and good. Great to make ahead, refrigerate, and let kids (or husbands!) heat in microwave for snacks or quick lunches.

LEE BUDD'S MEATLOAF

½ lb. Mozzarella cheese
2 lbs. lean ground beef
2 eggs
½ cup packaged seasoned
   bread crumbs
1 cup tomato juice
½ tsp. salt
1 tsp. oregano
Dash of pepper
2 small onions, minced
2 Tbsp. oil or butter
8 paper-thin slices ham

SERVES 8

Grate cheese and set aside. Combine beef, eggs, bread crumbs, tomato juice, salt, oregano, and pepper. Saute onion in oil or butter until golden, and add to meat mixture and blend. Turn out on a sheet of foil, and flatten out oblong to 1-inch thickness. Place ham slices on meat keeping 1 inch from edge. Sprinkle cheese on ham. Use foil to fold meat mixture over ham and cheese, closing all openings. Turn into loaf pan and pat into corners, shaping a loaf. Fill pan completely, rounding slightly on top. Bake at 325° for 60-75 minutes.

MEATS

HAMBURGER NOODLE BAKE

1 — 16 oz. pkg. noodles
2 lbs. hamburger
1 large onion, chopped
1 — 4 oz. can mushrooms,
    drained
2 — 10 oz. cans cream of
    chicken soup
1½ cups milk
½ tsp. salt
¼ tsp. pepper
¼ cup soy sauce
1 tsp. Worcestershire
    sauce
½ lb. Cheddar cheese,
    grated
½ cup mixed salted nuts,
    chopped
1½ cups crisp Chinese
    noodles

SERVES 8
Cook noodles in boiling, salted water. Drain well. Brown hamburger and onion; drain. Combine mushrooms, soup, and milk and add to meat mixture. Blend in spices and sauces. Put noodles in bottom of large casserole or Dutch oven; cover with meat mixture. Top with cheese. Bake at 350° for 15 minutes. Remove and top with nuts and Chinese noodles. Return to oven for 15 minutes longer.

JAPANESE BEEF AND VEGETABLES

½ cup blanched, slivered
 almonds
1 Tbsp. butter
¾ lb. ground beef
1 cup water
¼ tsp. salt
1 cup fine egg noodles
1 — 10 oz. pkg. Japanese
 style vegetables
1 Tbsp. soy sauce

SERVES 4
Saute almonds in butter until lightly browned. Remove from pan and set aside. Brown ground beef well in same skillet, leaving meat in chunks. Stir in water and salt and bring to a boil. Stir in noodles. Cover and simmer for 2 minutes. Add vegetables and bring to a full boil over medium heat, separating vegetables with a fork and stirring frequently. Cover and simmer for 3 minutes. Stir in soy sauce and sprinkle with almonds. Serve immediately.

Try this with Orange-Almond Salad for an Oriental style meal your family will love.

PRIZE PORK ROAST

1 — 4 or 5 lb. pork roast
1 tsp. salt
1 tsp. pepper (freshly
 ground is best)
1 tsp. dried thyme
2 carrots, peeled and cut in
 2-inch pieces
1 onion, sliced
2-3 stalks celery, sliced
Fresh parsley
1 bay leaf
1 — 10 oz. can beef
 consomme
¼ cup dry white wine
Juice of ½ lemon

SERVES 6
Preheat oven to 450°. Mix together salt, pepper, and thyme. Rub into roast. Put meat into roasting pan along with carrots, onion, parsley and bay leaf. Pour consomme and wine over roast. Brown at 450° for 20 minutes. Reduce heat to 350° and bake, uncovered for 3 hours. Add water as necessary during baking. Pour lemon juice over the roast five minutes before removing it from oven.

MEATS

TOMICHI RANCH HOLIDAY PORK ROAST

4-6 lb. pork shoulder roast, boned and rolled
1½ cups dried fruit, cut in chunks
1 tsp. salt
½ tsp. pepper
1½ cups water or apple juice

GRAVY:
¼-½ cup flour
¾ cup reserved fruit juice
Pan drippings

SERVES 6-8

Combine dried fruit and water or juice in a small saucepan and bring to boil. Reduce heat and simmer until all of the fruit is tender; drain fruit reserving juice.

Unroll roast and spread the fruit over the meat. Roll and retie the roast. Sprinkle the salt and pepper over the meat. Insert a meat thermometer and roast at 350° in a covered pan for approximately 30 minutes per pound, or until thermometer reaches 185°. Remove lid during last ½ hour of roasting time.

Remove roast from pan and make a gravy mixing flour with reserved fruit juice in a lidded jar. Shake until mixed well and stir into pan drippings. Bring to a slow boil, adding water if necessary to make desired consistency. Slice roast and serve with gravy.

This can be such a special Christmas dinner!

APRICOT GLAZED HAM

1 — 5 lb. fully cooked, smoked ham
⅓ cup brown sugar, firmly packed
¼ cup apricot preserves
1 tsp. dry mustard

SERVES 8

Score top of ham in a diamond design. Mix brown sugar, preserves, and dry mustard well. Coat top and sides of ham with mixture. Bake, uncovered, at 325° for 1½ hours.

CAJUN STUFFED PORK CHOPS

4 pork chops, 1½ inch
  thick
1 tsp. salt
¼ tsp. black pepper
¼-½ tsp. cayenne
¼ tsp. ground mustard
½ tsp. dried thyme
2 Tbsp. butter or margarine
1 onion, finely chopped
1 garlic clove, peeled and
  minced
½ cup green pepper,
  chopped
1 cup ground ham
½ cup cornbread stuffing
1 large egg, beaten

SERVES 4

Lay pork chops in a baking dish. Sprinkle with mixture of salt, pepper, cayenne, mustard, and thyme. Reserve any left over spice mixture. Broil pork chops to brown.

Melt butter in skillet and cook onion, garlic, and green pepper until softened. Remove from heat and mix in ham, cornbread, egg, and reserved spices. Mound dressing mixture on top of each pork chop and bake uncovered at 375° for 1 hour.

OVEN BARBECUED PORK CHOPS

6 pork chops
½ cup ketchup
1 tsp. celery seed
1 bay leaf
2 Tbsp. brown sugar
4 Tbsp. white vinegar
1 cup water
1 tsp. prepared mustard

SERVES 4-6

Brown pork chops in a skillet over medium high heat. Arrange in a 9 x 13 inch baking dish. Mix other ingredients in a small saucepan and heat through. Pour over chops and bake uncovered at 375° for 1 hour. If sauce starts getting thick, cover after 45 minutes.

MEATS

SWEET 'N SOUR SPARERIBS

2 lbs. pork spareribs (or
  country-style if you
  prefer)
½ tsp. salt
¼ tsp. garlic powder
½ cup sugar
¼ cup vinegar
¼ cup soy sauce
⅛ cup water
1 tsp. cornstarch
1 — 8 oz. can pineapple
  chunks, undrained

SERVES 4
Cut spareribs into desired pieces,
place in a 9 x 13 inch pan, and brown
uncovered in 350° oven for 45 minutes. Combine salt, garlic, sugar,
vinegar, and soy sauce in a small
saucepan. Heat to dissolve sugar.
Mix water and cornstarch and stir
into sauce. Heat to thicken slightly.
Stir in pineapple. Pour over ribs,
cover, reduce heat to 300°, and bake
2 additional hours.

Good with Egg Rolls!

EGG ROLLS

¼ lb. ground pork
½ cup chopped celery
1 bunch green onions,
  chopped
1 — 6 oz. can water
  chestnuts, diced
2 Tbsp. soy sauce
¾ lb. bean sprouts
1 tsp. cornstarch
12 egg roll wrappers
Oil for frying

MAKES 12
In a skillet, brown pork for 5-10 minutes. Drain grease. Add celery, onions, water chestnuts, and soy
sauce. Cook 2 minutes. Add bean
sprouts and cook another 2 minutes.
May add cornstarch to thicken if desired. Cool. Spoon into egg roll wrappers, folding them up like an envelope. Moisten edges to seal. Deep
fry at 360° in 1½ inches oil until
golden brown. Drain on paper towels
and serve warm.

ITALIAN SAUSAGE AND ZUCCHINI STIR FRY

1 lb. Italian sausage
½ cup chopped onions
2 chopped tomatoes
4 cups zucchini, sliced
   thinly
1 tsp. lemon juice
¼ tsp. salt
¼ tsp. Tabasco sauce
¼ tsp. oregano
Parmesan cheese

SERVES 4

Brown crumbled Italian sausage in a skillet. Add onions when sausage is nearly done. Drain fat. Add tomatoes, zucchini, lemon juice, salt, Tabasco sauce and oregano. Cook, uncovered for about 5 minutes, stirring frequently. Remove to serving plate; sprinkle with cheese. Serve with garlic bread.

MATT'S SWEET AND SOUR SAUSAGE

3 slices bacon, diced and
   cooked
8 oz. fully cooked smoked
   sausage, sliced into
   1 inch pieces
¼ cup chopped onion
¼ cup chopped green
   pepper
1 Tbsp. flour
1 Tbsp. sugar
½ tsp. dry mustard
½ tsp. celery seed
½ tsp. salt
½ cup water
¼ cup cider vinegar
4 medium potatoes,
   peeled, cooked, and
   sliced

SERVES 4-6

In a large skillet, brown bacon and sausage. Remove from skillet. In same skillet, saute onion and green pepper until tender. Stir in flour, sugar, mustard, celery seed, and salt. Add water and vinegar and cook until thickened. Add potatoes, sausage, and bacon and heat through.

Delicious!

MEATS

BARBECUED PORK RIBS

4 lbs. spareribs
Barbecue sauce

SERVES 4
Place ribs meaty side up in an open shallow roasting pan. Drizzle barbecue sauce over ribs. Roast at 325° for 1½ hours. Finish cooking outside on the grill for that charcoal flavor. Serve with fresh corn on the cob and a green salad for a summertime hit.

EASY & DELICIOUS PORK CHOP SUPPER

6 pork chops
Salt and pepper
5 cups favorite dressing,
    prepared
1-2 sweet potatoes, peeled
    and sliced into six
    1-inch slices

SERVES 4-6
Salt and pepper pork chops and place in a 9 x 13 inch baking dish. Brown in a 350° oven for 20 minutes. Drain grease. Place ¾ cup dressing on top of each pork chop; top with a slice of sweet potato. Cover and finish baking for 45 minutes.

This is so easy and tasty. Serve with a green salad or vegetable and your meal is complete!

SAVANNAH RED RICE

4 strips bacon
2 green peppers, chopped
2 medium onions, chopped
2 cups cooked rice
1 — 16 oz. can stewed
tomatoes, chopped
1 — 8 oz. can tomato sauce
1 tsp. Tabasco sauce
¼ cup Parmesan cheese
¼ tsp. pepper, or to taste
1 lb. Polish sausage, sliced
½-1 lb. shrimp and/or
imitation crab

SERVES 4-6

Fry bacon and set aside. Brown peppers and onions in bacon drippings. Add sausage and shrimp or crab. Saute for about 1-2 minutes until sausage is hot through. Add rice, tomatoes, tomato sauce, Tabasco, and crumbled bacon. Pour into greased 9 x 13 inch casserole. Sprinkle pepper and Parmesan on top. Bake at 325° for 30 minutes or until rice is dry enough to separate. Great served with a salad.

This was a big hit with the family…a nice change from hamburger and chicken.

CHICKEN AND FISH

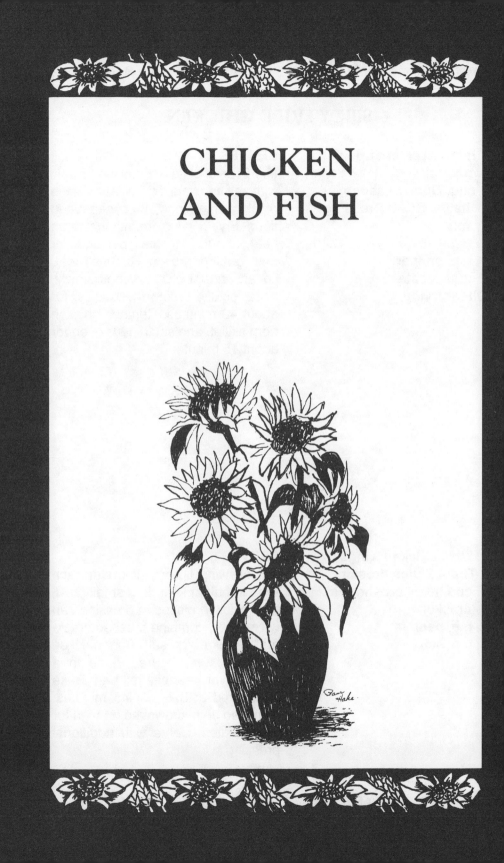

CHICKEN & FISH

SPICY FRIED CHICKEN

1 large fryer, cut up
1 cup flour
1 pkg. Good Seasons
　Italian Salad Dressing
　mix
½ tsp. salt
¼ tsp. pepper
2 eggs, beaten
Oil for frying

SERVES 4

Mix flour and Italian seasoning mix with salt and pepper. Roll each piece of chicken in egg, then seasoned flour. Fry in oil over medium high heat, about 3 minutes per side, or until golden brown. Reduce heat, cover, and let chicken cook slowly, occasionally turning the pieces, for about 40 minutes. Remove chicken from skillet, and set in 300° oven for about 15 minutes.

You can't beat fried chicken, and this version adds a nice new flavor to an old favorite.

RANCH WINGS

1½ lbs. chicken wings
2 Tbsp. Ranch dressing
⅔ cup finely crushed Ritz
　crackers
½ tsp. paprika
½ tsp. salt

SERVES 6

Cut off wing tips at joint. Cut each wing in half at joint. In a small bowl, toss chicken pieces in dressing. On wax paper, combine crushed crackers, paprika, and salt. Coat chicken with cracker mixture. Place in a single layer in a jelly roll pan. Bake uncovered at 375° for 45 minutes. Can also be microwaved on high for 7-9 minutes. Serve with additional dressing.

CHICKEN DRUMSTICKS

20-25 drumsticks (18 fit in a 9 x 13 inch pan)
1 cup water
1 cup soy sauce
1 cup sugar
¼ cup unsweetened pineapple juice
¼ cup oil
1 tsp. garlic powder
1 tsp. ginger

Mix water, soy sauce, sugar, pine-apple juice, oil and spices. Pour over drumsticks that have been placed in a 9 x 13 inch pan. Marinate in refrigerator overnight. Bake at 350° for 1 hour or until drumsticks are done. Remove from marinade. Serve cold.

This is a great dish to take on picnics. Can also be used as an appetizer.

CHICKEN IN THE GOLD

4 chicken breasts
1 cup honey
1 cup prepared mustard
1 tsp. curry powder

SERVES 4

Place chicken breasts in a 9 x 13 inch baking dish. Cook for about 25 minutes at 350°. While chicken is cooking, combine honey, mustard, and curry in a saucepan. Cook over medium-low heat for 15 minutes. Drain grease off chicken, then pour sauce over it. Let cook for an additional 15 minutes. Chicken is done when sauce is bubbly and slightly brown.

This easy supper dish is a delightful change from fried or plain baked chicken. Serve with rice and a vegetable. Great for family or company.

CHICKEN & FISH

DIJON-HERB CHICKEN

8 chicken breast halves,
  skinned and boned
¼ cup butter or margarine,
  melted
¼ cup lemon juice
2 Tbsp. Worcestershire
  sauce
1 Tbsp. Dijon mustard
½ tsp. salt
2 Tbsp. chopped fresh
  chives (½ Tbsp. dried)
2 Tbsp. chopped fresh
  parsley (½ Tbsp. dried)

SERVES 6-8
In a skillet, saute chicken in butter about 10 minutes on each side. Remove to a serving plate and keep warm. To reserved pan drippings, add lemon juice, Worcestershire, mustard, and salt. Bring to a boil, stirring. Stir in herbs. Pour over chicken and serve.

Good with rice...makes a quick and easy supper.

BAKED PECAN CHICKEN

1 chicken, cut into pieces
1 cup Bisquick
½ cup chopped pecans
1 tsp. paprika
1 tsp. salt
1 tsp. poultry seasoning
1 cup sour cream, or
  ½ cup evaporated milk
¼ cup butter, melted

SERVES 4
Mix Bisquick, pecans, paprika, salt, and poultry seasoning. Spread sour cream over chicken. Roll in Bisquick mix. Place chicken, skin side up, not touching, in greased baking dish. Sprinkle with remaining mix and drizzle with butter. Bake, uncovered, at 400° for 40 minutes.

CHICKEN VERMOUTH

6 chicken breast halves
1 — 10.5 oz. can cream of
   chicken soup
1 — 10.5 oz. can cream of
   mushroom soup
1 — 10.5 oz. can cream of
   celery soup
½ cup dry vermouth
¼ cup Parmesan cheese
1 pkg. sliced almonds

SERVES 4-6
Place chicken in a 9 x 13 inch casserole. Mix remaining ingredients and pour over chicken. Bake, uncovered, at 350° for about 1 hour and 15 minutes. Serve with hot rice.

CHICKEN FIESTA

1 cup Cheddar cheese
   cracker crumbs
2 Tbsp. taco seasoning mix
8 chicken breast halves,
   skinned and boned
4 green onions, chopped
2 Tbsp. butter or
   margarine, melted
2 cups whipping cream
1 cup Monterey Jack
   cheese, grated
1 cup Cheddar cheese,
   grated
1 — 4 oz. can chopped
   green chilies
½ tsp. chicken-flavored
   bouillon granules

SERVES 8
Combine cracker crumbs and taco seasoning. Dredge chicken breasts in crumbs and place in a greased 9 x 13 inch baking dish.

Saute green onions in butter in a skillet until tender. Stir in whipping cream and remaining ingredients. Pour over chicken. Sprinkle remaining crumb mixture on top. Bake, uncovered, at 350° for 45 minutes.

CHICKEN & FISH

CHINESE CHICKEN

6 chicken breast halves
½ cup butter or margarine, melted
½ cup soy sauce
4 Tbsp. Worcestershire sauce

SERVES 4-6

Arrange chicken in a Pyrex baking dish. Combine melted butter, soy sauce, and Worcestershire. Pour over chicken and bake at 350° for 1 hour, basting chicken with sauce during cooking time. Can also be cooked on the grill.

Great flavor!

ARIZONA CHICKEN

4 chicken breast halves
1 — 16 oz. can whole tomatoes
1 large onion, chopped
½ tsp. garlic powder
2 Tbsp. chili powder
½ tsp. oregano
¼ cup white wine
Salt and pepper
2 cups cooked rice

SERVES 4

Place chicken in a baking dish. Blend tomatoes, onion, garlic powder, chili powder, oregano and white wine. Pour over chicken and bake at 350°, covered, for 1 hour. Can be cooked in a crockpot on low all day. Serve over hot cooked rice.

CHAMPIONSHIP CHICKEN

6 chicken breast filets
6 slices Swiss cheese
1 cup cream of chicken soup
¼ cup milk
2 cups seasoned stuffing mix
⅓ cup butter, melted

SERVES 6

In a greased 9 x 13 inch casserole, lay chicken breasts meaty side up. Put a slice of cheese on each piece. Mix soup and milk and pour over chicken. Sprinkle stuffing mix over all. Pour melted butter over top and bake at 350° for 1 hour.

CHICKEN & FISH

ITALIAN SKILLET CHICKEN

4 boneless, skinless
  chicken breast halves
8 Tbsp. grated Parmesan
  cheese
3 Tbsp. flour
Salt and pepper to taste
2 Tbsp. olive oil
1 cup sliced mushrooms
½ onion, finely chopped
½ tsp. rosemary, crushed
¼ tsp. garlic powder
½ tsp. leaf basil
1 — 14½ oz. can Italian-
  style stewed tomatoes
Cooked pasta

SERVES 4

Coat each chicken breast in cheese, then flour. Salt and pepper to taste. In skillet, cook chicken in oil over medium high heat until done. Remove to serving platter and keep warm.

In same skillet, cook mushrooms, onion, rosemary, garlic, and basil until soft. Add tomatoes and cook uncovered until thickened. Spoon over chicken and top with remaining Parmesan cheese. Serve over cooked pasta.

CHICKEN PARMESAN

4 chicken breast halves,
  boneless, skinless
¾ cup bread crumbs
6 Tbsp. Parmesan cheese
2 eggs, lightly beaten
Vegetable oil
8 oz. Mozzarella cheese,
  sliced
1 — 16 oz. jar spaghetti
  sauce
Garlic salt

SERVES 4

Pound chicken to ¼-inch thickness. Mix bread crumbs and 4 Tbsp. Parmesan. Dip chicken in egg, then bread crumb mixture. In a large skillet, heat oil (about 3-4 tablespoons), and brown the chicken on both sides. Remove from skillet and place in a 9 x 13 inch baking dish. Place a slice of Mozzarella cheese on each piece, then pour spaghetti sauce over. Sprinkle with remaining Parmesan and garlic salt. Bake at 350° until hot and bubbly, about 15 minutes. Broil for a few minutes to brown.

153

CHICKEN & FISH

CRANBERRY CHICKEN

2-3 lbs. boneless chicken
  breasts
1 — 16 oz. can whole
  cranberry sauce
1 small bottle French
  dressing
1 envelope dry onion soup
  mix

SERVES 4-6
Place chicken in a baking dish. Mix cranberry sauce, dressing, and onion soup mix. Blend well. Pour over chicken. Cover and bake at 325° for 1 hour. Uncover and bake for 15 more minutes. Serve over rice.

This easy, sweet and sour chicken can also be done in a slow cooker. Place all ingredients in cooker and cook on low all day.

SOUTHWESTERN GRILLED CHICKEN

2 medium tomatoes,
  quartered
2 cups chopped onion
½ cup chopped red bell
  pepper
4 garlic cloves or 1 tsp.
  garlic powder
¼ cup fresh cilantro leaves
⅔ cup soy sauce
6 Tbsp. oil
2 Tbsp. fresh lime juice
1 tsp. black pepper
10 boneless chicken
  breasts
Fresh parsley, chopped

SERVES 10
Place tomatoes, onions, pepper, garlic, cilantro, soy sauce, oil, lime juice and black pepper in a food processor or blender, and process for 30 seconds. Pour this marinade over the chicken breasts, and marinate, covered and refrigerated for at least 4 hours turning frequently. Remove chicken from the marinade and grill over medium coals for 20-30 minutes, turning frequently and basting with marinade. Sprinkle with parsley before serving.

FANNY WARREN'S CURRIED CHICKEN CREPES

CREPE BATTER:
1 cup presifted flour
2 eggs
½ cup milk
½ cup water
¼ tsp. salt
2 Tbsp. butter or
   margarine, melted

CHICKEN FILLING:
4 Tbsp. butter or margarine
1 medium onion, chopped
1 cup finely diced celery
2 Tbsp. flour
½ tsp. salt
¼ tsp. pepper
2 tsp. curry powder
1 cup chicken broth
3 cups diced cooked
   chicken
½ cup sour cream

GARNISH:
Chutney
Chopped peanuts
Shredded coconut
Bacon bits

MAKES 16
Place batter ingredients in blender or food processor in order given. Blend 30 seconds, stop and stir down sides. Blend another 30-60 seconds until smooth. (Can be mixed by hand with wire whisk or mixer. First combine flour and eggs, then add liquid gradually, blending until smooth.) It is important to measure flour and liquid carefully since consistency of batter is a key to good crepes. Batter can be used immediately, or refrigerated to three days for use as needed.

Heat a lightly greased 6-inch skillet. Remove from heat; spoon in about 2 tablespoons batter. Lift and tilt skillet to spread batter evenly. Return to heat; brown on one side only. Invert pan and gently remove crepe with a fork. Repeat with remaining batter, greasing skillet occasionally.

To make filling, melt butter in a large skillet; add onion and celery and saute until just tender-crisp. Stir in flour and seasonings and cook 5 minutes. Add broth and bring to simmer until thickened. Remove from heat and stir in chicken and cream. Place heaping tablespoon or two of mixture across center of each crepe, brown side out. Roll and place seam side down in buttered 9 x 13 inch baking pan. Bake 20-25 minutes at 375° until hot and bubbling. Garnish as desired.

155

QUICK CHICKEN BURRITOS

**6 chicken breast filets,
    chopped
2-3 Tbsp. butter
½ onion, chopped
1 — 4 oz. can chopped
    green chilies
1 — 10 oz. can cream of
    chicken soup
6-8 flour tortillas
6-8 strips Monterey Jack
    cheese**

SERVES 6

Saute chicken pieces in melted butter. Add onion and cook until chicken is cooked through and onion is translucent. Add chilies (to taste) and soup. Mix well and heat through.

Warm flour tortillas. Add a strip of cheese to each tortilla, then spoon chicken mixture into tortilla. Roll and serve immediately.

Kids love this burrito-style meal, and it is so fast and easy, the cook will love it, too!

MEXICAN SKILLET CHICKEN

**5 Tbsp. oil
3 — 8-inch flour tortillas,
    cut into ½ inch strips
2 whole chicken breasts,
    skinned, boned, cut into
    ½ inch strips
½ cup diced onions
¼ cup chopped green
    and/or red pepper
1 — 10 oz. pkg. frozen corn
1 — 8 oz. jar thick and
    chunky salsa**

SERVES 4

Heat 3 tablespoons oil in a large skillet over medium-high heat until hot. Add tortilla strips, a few at a time; cook for 1 to 2 minutes or until crisp, stirring constantly. Place crisp tortilla strips on paper towel to drain.

Add remaining 2 tablespoons oil to skillet. Add chicken strips, onion, and pepper; cook until chicken is browned and no longer pink, stirring constantly. Stir in corn and salsa. Bring to a boil. Reduce heat to low; simmer uncovered 5 minutes or until corn is heated. Stir in tortilla strips. Serve immediately.

ARROZ CON POLLO

2 lbs. chicken pieces
3 Tbsp. flour
½ tsp. salt
¼ cup oil
1 cup long-grain rice
½ cup onion, chopped
1 — 14½ oz. can stewed
   tomatoes
1 cup chicken broth
1 — 4 oz. can chopped
   green chilies
1 tsp. garlic powder
½ tsp. ground cumin
¼ tsp. pepper
½ tsp. salt

SERVES 6
Mix flour and salt in a plastic bag. Shake chicken pieces in bag until coated. Heat oil in a skillet. Brown chicken pieces in oil; drain on paper towels. Saute rice and onions in drippings until rice is golden. Stir in remaining ingredients. Transfer to a 9 x 13 inch baking dish. Arrange chicken pieces on rice. Cover and bake at 350° for about one hour, or until liquid is absorbed and chicken is done.

GREEN CHILE CHICKEN

1 large fryer, cooked and
   boned
1 cup chopped onion
1 — 10 oz. can cream of
   mushroom soup
1 — 10 oz. can green chile
   enchilada sauce
½ cup chicken broth
2-3 Tbsp. green chilies,
   chopped
12 corn tortillas, torn into
   pieces (can substitute
   with packaged tortilla
   chips)
½ lb. Cheddar cheese,
   grated (can substitute
   Monterey Jack)

SERVES 8
Cook chicken in boiling, salted water until tender. Save stock. Bone chicken and cut into pieces. Mix onion, soup, enchilada sauce, broth and green chilies in a bowl. Grease a 2 quart casserole and place a layer of soup mixture, then chicken pieces, then grated cheese. Repeat, ending with cheese. Bake at 350°, uncovered for 45 minutes.

CHICKEN FAJITAS

2 Tbsp. lemon juice
½ tsp. salt
½ tsp. liquid smoke
¼ tsp. pepper
¼ tsp. garlic powder
4 chicken breast halves,
   skinned, boned, and cut
   into strips
2 Tbsp. oil
1 green (or red) bell
   pepper, seeded and cut
   into strips
1 medium onion, sliced
8 flour tortillas

SERVES 4

Combine first 5 ingredients. Add chicken and stir to coat. Cover and refrigerate at least 30 minutes, overnight is fine. Drain chicken; reserve marinade.

Heat oil in a skillet. Add chicken and cook 2-3 minutes, stirring. Add marinade, peppers, and onion. Saute until vegetables are crisp-tender. Divide mixture evenly among the warmed tortillas, wrap and serve immediately. Can be garnished with chopped tomato, lettuce, green onion, guacamole, grated cheese, sour cream or picante. However, these are terrific just plain!

CHICKEN TETTRAZINI

1 onion, chopped
1 cup chopped celery
3 Tbsp. margarine or butter
1 chicken, boiled, boned,
   and cut up
1 cup chicken broth
8 oz. cooked spaghetti,
   broken in 2-inch pieces
½ cup milk
1 — 10 oz. can cream of
   mushroom soup

TOPPING:
½ cup Parmesan cheese
2 Tbsp. parsley flakes

SERVES 6

Saute onions and celery in margarine. Combine chicken, broth, spaghetti, milk, and soup with sauteed vegetables, and place in a 9 x 13 inch greased baking dish. Top with Parmesan and parsley. Bake, uncovered, at 350° for 45-60 minutes.

CHICKEN & FISH

CHICKEN AND SEAFOOD ENCHILADAS

12 corn tortillas
1 medium onion, chopped
1 — 4 oz. can chopped
 green chilies
1 cup cooked chicken
1 lb. medium cooked
 shrimp
½ cup black olives, sliced
½-1 cup cooked scallops
½ lb. Monterey Jack
 cheese, grated
½ lb. Longhorn cheese,
 grated
1 cup light cream
½ cup sour cream
¼ cup butter
¾ tsp. oregano
½ tsp. garlic powder

GARNISH:
1 avocado, sliced
1 small jar pimento slices
¼ cup green and black
 olives, sliced

SERVES 6-8

Butter a 9 x 13 inch dish and line with half the tortillas. Layer half the onion, chilies, chicken, shrimp, scallops, olives in that order. Combine cheeses; reserve ¾ cup; sprinkle half over the olives.

Mix cream, sour cream, butter, oregano, and garlic powder and heat until blended. Pour half of sauce over cheese.

Repeat layering. Bake uncovered for an hour at 350° or until casserole is bubbly. Turn oven to 450°; sprinkle with remaining ¾ cup cheese and bake 5 minutes. Garnish if desired.

CHICKEN & FISH

CHICKEN BOBOLI

1 — 16 oz. Boboli pizza
   crust
4 boneless fryer breasts
2-3 Tbsp. cooking oil
1 onion, chopped
1 green pepper, chopped
½ lb. mushrooms, sliced
½ cup ripe olives, sliced
1 tsp. garlic salt
1 tsp. oregano
1 — 16 oz. jar Prego pizza
   sauce
2 cups grated Mozzarella
   cheese

SERVES 4-6
Cut chicken into 1-inch pieces. In a large frying pan, heat cooking oil. Saute chicken, onion, green pepper, mushrooms, olives. Cook about 5 minutes or until chicken is done. Add garlic salt and oregano. Place Boboli crust on a pizza pan. Spread pizza sauce over crust. Spoon chicken mixture evenly over sauce. Top with Mozzarella and bake at 425° for 10-15 minutes or until Mozzarella is browned and sauce is bubbly. Boboli crusts are great for any homemade pizza toppings, but we particularly like this one...it is easy and different. Try it!

MELT IN YOUR MOUTH CHICKEN PIE

1 — 3 lb. fryer
2 cups reserved chicken
   broth
1 — 10 oz. can cream of
   chicken soup
1 cup self-rising flour
1 tsp. salt
½ tsp. black pepper
1 cup buttermilk
1 stick margarine, melted

SERVES 6
Cook chicken until tender. Remove meat and skin from bones and dice. Reserve broth. Place diced chicken in a 9 x 13 inch pan. In a saucepan, bring to a boil the broth and soup. In another bowl, combine flour, salt, pepper, buttermilk and margarine. Mix thoroughly to make a batter. Pour broth mixture over chicken. Spoon batter over top. Bake at 425° for 25-30 minutes.

CHICKEN DUMPLETS

4 tsp. flour
4 tsp. butter
1 cup evaporated milk
2 cups chicken broth
2 — 8 oz. pkgs. cream
  cheese
1 tsp. salt
½ tsp. pepper
1 — 4.5 oz. can ripe olives,
  sliced
1 — 2.5 oz. can sliced
  mushrooms, drained
4 cups cooked chicken,
  diced
4 cups egg noodles,
  cooked and drained
Sliced almonds

SERVES 8-10
Combine flour, butter, milk and chicken stock in a saucepan. Stir until creamy and thickened. Cube cream cheese and add to white sauce. Stir until melted. Blend in salt, pepper, drained olives, and mushrooms. Fold in chicken and noodles. Transfer mixture into a 9 x 13 inch baking dish. Top with sliced almonds. Bake at 350° for 30 minutes.

GRILLED CATFISH

3 lbs. catfish filets
⅓ cup lemon juice
⅓ cup olive oil
1 clove garlic, minced
1 tsp. salt
Dash of Tabasco
1½ tsp. dry mustard
½ tsp. sweet basil
¼ tsp. pepper

SERVES 6-8
Combine olive oil and lemon juice. Add all remaining spices to mixture. Pour over catfish. Marinate for 5 minutes. Remove fish from marinade. Grill for 4-5 minutes on each side over moderately hot coals. Turn as needed and baste often with marinade.

CHICKEN & FISH

OVERNIGHT CRAB CASSEROLE

1 lb. fresh lump crabmeat
3 green onions and tops,
  chopped
Juice of 1 lemon
1 cup Velveeta cheese,
  grated
3 cups French bread, cut in
  1-inch cubes
5 Tbsp. butter, melted
1¾ cups milk
3 eggs, beaten
3 drops hot pepper sauce
½ tsp. dry mustard

SERVES 6-8

Toss crabmeat lightly with onions, lemon juice, and cheese. In a buttered 1½ quart casserole, arrange alternating layers of bread drizzled with melted butter and cheese/crab mixture. Combine remaining ingredients. Pour over crab mixture, cover and refrigerate overnight. Remove from refrigerator 1 hour before baking. Bake, covered, at 350° for 30 minutes. Uncover and finish baking (approximately 30 minutes more). Casserole will be puffed and golden brown. Cut in squares to serve.

This is a nice luncheon recipe.

BLEND OF THE BAYOU

1 — 8 oz. pkg. cream
  cheese
1 stick butter or margarine
1 — 10½ oz. can cream of
  mushroom soup
1 onion, chopped
1 bell pepper, chopped
3 ribs celery, chopped
1 Tbsp. butter
2 — 6½ oz. cans crabmeat
1 to 2 lbs. peeled,
  deveined, and chopped
  shrimp
2-3 cups cooked rice
Tabasco sauce to taste
Cracker crumbs
Grated Cheddar cheese

SERVES 10-12

Soften cream cheese and mix with butter and mushroom soup until smooth and there are no lumps. Saute chopped vegetables in 1 tablespoon butter until tender. Mix together cream cheese mixture, vegetables, crab, shrimp, rice, and Tabasco. Place in casserole, top with cheese and cracker crumbs. Bake about 30 to 45 minutes at 350°.

This Louisiana-style recipe is one of those you can make to taste by adding crushed red peppers, more cheese, etc.

HADDOCK SUPREME

2 lbs. haddock steaks, 1-
  inch thick
½ cup mayonnaise
½ cup sour cream
2 tsp. flour
1½ tsp. lemon juice
1 Tbsp. minced onion
⅛ tsp. cayenne pepper
½ cup shredded Cheddar
  cheese

SERVES 4-6
Rinse haddock steaks and pat dry. Arrange steaks side by side in a greased 8 x 12 inch baking dish. In small bowl, combine mayonnaise, sour cream and flour, stirring until smooth. Stir in lemon juice, onion and cayenne. Spoon mixture evenly over fish to cover completely. Bake uncovered at 425° for 20-25 minutes. Sprinkle cheese over fish and continue to bake until cheese is just melted, about 2 minutes. Serve with wild rice and a green salad.

Can also use halibut in this easy, tasty fish entree.

GOLDEN FRIED OYSTERS

1 quart large oysters
¼ cup milk
2 eggs, beaten
1 cup flour
1½ cups seasoned fish
  breading (Shake 'n
  Bake)
Oil for frying

SERVES 6
Drain oysters. Combine eggs and milk. Combine flour and fish breading. Roll oysters in flour mixture. Dip in milk and egg mixture, then again in flour mixture. Fry in very hot oil until golden brown.

CHICKEN & FISH

SCALLOPS IN VEGETABLES

2 cups sliced zucchini
1½ cups mushrooms,
   halved
1 lb. scallops, halved
¼ cup butter, melted
1 Tbsp. minced fresh
   parsley
¼ tsp. salt
¼ tsp. dried whole dillweed
Dash of pepper
3 Tbsp. lemon juice

SERVES 4

Cover zucchini with boiling water; let stand 5 minutes. Drain. Place zucchini in a 9 x 13 inch baking dish. Add mushrooms and top with scallops. Combine butter and remaining ingredients; spoon over scallops. Cover with aluminum foil and bake at 350° for 30 minutes or until done.

This recipe can also be baked in individual oven-proof baking dishes. Just divide amounts equally four ways, cover each dish, and bake as directed.

FRESH SCALLOPS IN WINE

1 lb. fresh scallops
¼ cup butter or margarine,
   melted
½ cup sliced fresh
   mushrooms
¼ cup chopped onion
¼ tsp. garlic powder
½ cup dry white wine
3 Tbsp. lemon juice
3 Tbsp. lime juice
½ tsp. dried whole oregano
½ tsp. celery salt
¼ tsp. pepper
Hot cooked vermicelli
Chopped fresh parsley

SERVES 4

Saute scallops in butter in a large skillet 3 minutes or until tender. Remove scallops from skillet, reserving drippings. Saute mushrooms, onion, and garlic 3 to 5 minutes; remove vegetables, reserve drippings. Add wine, juices, and seasonings to skillet. Bring to a boil, and cook 8 minutes. Stir in scallops and vegetables; cook until heated through. Serve over hot vermicelli. Garnish with chopped fresh parsley, if desired.

SHRIMP SOUTH LOUISIANA

2 lbs. raw shrimp, peeled
5 Tbsp. shortening
¼ cup flour
1 large onion, chopped
6 green onions, chopped
¼ cup green pepper,
   chopped
½ cup celery, chopped
¼ tsp. garlic powder
1 — 10 oz. can Ro-Tel
   tomatoes
1 — 8 oz. can tomato sauce
Salt and pepper to taste
1 Tbsp. Worcestershire
   sauce
Cooked rice

SERVES 4

Wash shrimp well and set aside. In a heavy saucepan, make a roux by heating shortening with flour. Cook on medium heat, stirring constantly, until dark brown. Add chopped onions, pepper, celery and garlic. Add Ro-Tel tomatoes and tomato sauce. Season with salt, pepper, and Worcestershire sauce. Let simmer, covered, about 30 minutes. Bring to boiling point, add shrimp. Cook 20 minutes. Serve over cooked rice.

This delicious Cajun-style recipe is very spicy, so if you like shrimp and you like hot-pepper flavored sauce, you'll love this!

CHICKEN & FISH

SHRIMP LO MEIN

2 Tbsp. oil
1 lb. fresh medium-sized
  uncooked shrimp,
  shelled, deveined
1 — 14.5 oz. can chicken
  broth
3 Tbsp. soy sauce
1 tsp. sugar
¼ tsp. ginger
¼ tsp. garlic powder
1½ cups uncooked fine
  egg noodles
1 medium onion, cut into
  eight wedges
1 — 10 oz. box frozen
  chopped broccoli
2 carrots, thinly sliced
1 can water chestnuts,
  drained and sliced
2 tsp. cornstarch
2 Tbsp. water

SERVES 5

Heat oil in large skillet or wok over medium-high heat until hot. Add shrimp; cook and stir 2-3 minutes or until shrimp are firm and pink. Remove shrimp from skillet; keep warm. Add chicken broth, soy sauce, sugar, ginger and garlic powder to skillet. Bring to a boil. Add egg noodles, onion, broccoli, carrots, and water chestnuts; return to boiling. Reduce heat to low; cover and simmer 8-10 minutes or until egg noodles and vegetables are tender. Stir in shrimp.

In a small bowl, stir cornstarch into water until dissolved. Gradually stir into mixture in skillet. Cook and stir over medium-high heat until sauce is bubbly and thickened.

SOLE PROVENCAL

1 cup chopped onion
½ cup diced celery
¼ cup vegetable oil
1 — 16 oz. can tomatoes,
  cut up
2 Tbsp. chopped parsley
2 bay leaves
1¼ tsp. salt
¼ tsp. pepper
1 lb. sole filets

SERVES 4

In a large skillet, saute onion and celery in oil until tender. Add tomatoes, parsley, bay leaves, salt and pepper. Cover and simmer 20 minutes. Add sole filets and continue cooking for 10 minutes, or until fish flakes easily with a fork. Remove fish to warm platter. Spoon sauce over top of fish. Serve with rice.

VEGETABLES,
RICE
AND PASTA

VEGETABLES, RICE & PASTA

HERB GARDEN ASPARAGUS

1½ lbs. fresh asparagus
4 Tbsp. butter
2 cloves garlic, minced
1 tsp. fresh chives
1 Tbsp. chopped fresh
  parsley
1 Tbsp. lemon juice
¼ tsp. salt

SERVES 4

Add asparagus to boiling salted water. Cook until just tender, about 3 minutes. Drain. Melt butter in a small skillet and saute garlic, chives, and parsley. Add lemon juice and salt. Heat through. Pour over asparagus and serve immediately.

ASPARAGUS CAESAR

1 tsp. garlic powder
2 Tbsp. Dijon mustard
1 Tbsp. fresh lemon juice
1 tsp. Worcestershire
  sauce
¼ tsp. Tabasco
¼ cup olive oil
¼ cup Parmesan cheese
Salt and pepper to taste
1 lb. fresh asparagus
Purchased croutons
Parmesan cheese

SERVES 4

Add first five ingredients to blender or food processor. With machine running, gradually add oil. Add ¼ cup Parmesan. Season to taste with salt and pepper.

Add asparagus to boiling, salted water. Cook until just tender, about 3 minutes. Drain. Arrange asparagus spears on a platter. Drizzle with dressing and sprinkle with croutons and Parmesan.

NACHO BEAN BAKE

1 — 30 oz. can refried
  beans
1 — 17 oz. can whole corn,
  drained
1 — 14½ oz. can stewed
  tomatoes
1 — 4 oz. can chopped
  green chilies
1 — 2½ oz. can sliced
  black olives, drained
2 Tbsp. green onions,
  chopped
½ tsp. chili powder
½ tsp. garlic powder
½ tsp. ground cumin
4 cups crushed tortilla
  chips
2 cups Cheddar cheese,
  shredded

SERVES 8
In a bowl, combine first nine ingredients. On the bottom of a lightly greased 11 x 7½ x 2 inch baking dish, place 2 cups crushed tortilla chips. Top with bean mixture. Sprinkle remaining chips over beans, top with cheese. Bake at 350° for 20-25 minutes.

BUCKAROO BEANS

1 gallon canned pinto
  beans
1 envelope Lipton golden
  onion soup mix
1 — 14½ oz. can stewed
  tomatoes
1 whole Anaheim chile
  pepper

SERVES 12-15
Mix beans, soup mix, and stewed tomatoes in a large Dutch oven or stew pot. Place the pepper on top of the beans. Cover and simmer for 1 hour. Remove pepper and serve.

These beans are great for picnics or camp outs. They are better the second day as flavors have blended. Do not cook them for more than an hour or the beans will get mushy. Pepper is optional, but adds a zippy flavor.

BROCCOLI-CHEESE CASSEROLE

4 lbs. frozen chopped
   broccoli
Salt and pepper to taste
1 lb. Velveeta cheese,
   sliced
2 rolls Ritz crackers
1 stick margarine or butter,
   melted

SERVES 12

Cook broccoli in boiling water, drain, season with salt and pepper. Layer half of broccoli in a 9 x 13 inch baking dish. Place half of sliced Velveeta over. Crumble one roll of Ritz crackers on top of cheese. Repeat layers. Pour melted butter over all. Bake 20 minutes at 350°.

This wonderful vegetable dish is great for a crowd and so easy, too!

BROCCOLI WITH MORNAY SAUCE

3 — 10 oz. pkg. frozen
   chopped broccoli
3 slices white bread
2 Tbsp. butter

MORNAY SAUCE:
2 Tbsp. butter
2 Tbsp. flour
Salt to taste
⅛ tsp. cayenne pepper
1 tsp. Dijon mustard
1 cup milk
¼ cup Parmesan cheese,
   grated

SERVES 6-8

Grease a 2 quart casserole dish. Cook broccoli according to package directions and drain well. Cut bread into ½-inch cubes for croutons. Melt butter in a large skillet over medium heat. Saute bread cubes in skillet until lightly browned. Prepare Mornay sauce. Mix chopped broccoli with croutons and put into prepared baking dish. Top with Mornay Sauce and broil until lightly browned.

To prepare Mornay Sauce, melt butter in a small saucepan over low heat. Whisk in flour. Cook and stir 2-3 minutes. Add salt, red pepper and mustard. Gradually whisk in milk. Continue to whisk over medium heat until mixture is slightly thickened. Stir in cheese until melted.

BAKED CABBAGE

1 head cabbage, chopped
2 Tbsp. salt
1 — 10.5 oz. can cream of
   mushroom soup
¾ cup milk
1 cup grated Cheddar
   cheese
1 cup buttered bread
   crumbs

SERVES 4-6
Boil cabbage in salted water for 5 minutes. Drain. Combine soup, milk, and cheese. Stir into cabbage. Place in buttered 1½ quart casserole. Top with bread crumbs and bake, uncovered, at 350° for 20-30 minutes.

HONEY GLAZED CARROTS

3 cups carrots, sliced
¼ cup water
¼ cup honey
2 Tbsp. butter or margarine
2 Tbsp. parsley flakes
Salt to taste

SERVES 6
Cook carrots in water until tender. Drain. Stir in remaining ingredients until carrots are coated. Serve immediately.

CORN AND CHEESE PIE

3 large eggs
1 — 8.5 oz. can cream corn
1 — 8 oz. can whole corn,
   drained
1 stick margarine, melted
½ cup cornmeal
1 cup sour cream
4 oz. Monterey Jack
   cheese, shredded
4 oz. sharp Cheddar
   cheese, shredded
2 Tbsp. chopped green
   chilies
½ tsp. salt
¼ tsp. Worcestershire
   sauce

SERVES 6
Beat eggs and add rest of ingredients. Pour into a lightly greased 9-inch pie pan. Bake at 350° for 45-55 minutes or until firm and browned. Let rest 10 minutes before serving. Can be stored in refrigerator for 3 days or 3 months in freezer. If frozen, thaw and reheat at 350° for 20 minutes.

Delicious with a fresh fruit salad.

VEGETABLES, RICE & PASTA

CORN 'N OKRA

1 lb. okra (fresh is best,
   frozen will work)
1 cup corn kernels
3 Tbsp. bacon drippings
1 medium onion, chopped
1 large tomato, chopped
Salt and pepper to taste
1 cup beef broth

SERVES 4-6

Cut stems from okra, then slice pods into ¾ inch rounds. Heat bacon drippings in a large skillet. Add okra, corn, onion, and tomato. Fry for about 5 minutes, stirring often. Add salt and pepper. Reduce heat and add just enough broth to keep vegetables from sticking. Cover and cook for 20-25 minutes, stirring in more broth as needed.

If you enjoy the good Southern flavor of okra, you will find this tasty combination a real treat.

CORN ZUCCHINI BAKE

3 medium zucchini
¼ cup onion, chopped
1 Tbsp. butter
1 — 10 oz. pkg. frozen
   whole kernel corn,
   cooked and drained
1 cup Swiss cheese, grated
2 eggs, beaten
¼ tsp. salt
¼ cup bread crumbs
2 Tbsp. Parmesan cheese
1 Tbsp. butter, melted
½ cup tomato, chopped
Chopped parsley

SERVES 6

Cut unpeeled zucchini into 1-inch slices. Saute onion in 1 tablespoon butter until tender. Combine zucchini, onion, cooked corn, cheese, eggs, and salt. Turn mixture into 1-quart greased casserole dish. Combine crumbs, Parmesan, and melted butter. Sprinkle over corn mixture. Bake, uncovered, at 350° until knife inserted in center comes out clean, about 40 minutes. Garnish with chopped tomato and parsley.

VEGETABLES, RICE & PASTA

GREEN CHILE CASSEROLE

1 lb. medium Cheddar
  cheese, grated
2 — 4 oz. cans diced green
  chilies
1 pint sour cream
1 medium onion, chopped
2 — 10 oz. cans cream of
  mushroom soup
1 — 16 oz. bag tortilla
  chips

SERVES 10-12
Mix first five ingredients in a large mixing bowl. Add tortilla chips. Pour into 9 x 13 inch baking dish. Bake at 350° for about 30 minutes or until bubbly. Makes a great accompaniment for Mexican food.

EGGPLANT WITH CHEESE

1 lb. eggplant, peeled and
  cut crosswise in ½ inch
  slices
1 cup chicken broth
2 slices onion
12 blanched almonds,
  lightly toasted
Salt
2 slices mild cheese, such
  as Muenster or
  Jarlsberg
1 Tbsp. Parmesan cheese
Pepper
Nutmeg

SERVES 4
Place the eggplant slices in a pan with the broth and the onion slices. Simmer until the eggplant is just tender. Remove the eggplant to an ovenproof dish, reserving broth.

In a food processor or blender, chop the almonds fine. With the motor running, pour in ½ cup reserved broth, add water if necessary to make ½ cup. Salt to taste. Pour the liquid over the eggplant, cover with the slices of cheese, sprinkle with Parmesan, pepper and nutmeg. Bake, uncovered, at 350° for 20 minutes.

VEGETABLES, RICE & PASTA

RATATOUILLE

1 cup chopped onions
½ cup chopped green bell
   pepper
1 clove garlic, minced
2 Tbsp. oil
1 small zucchini, thinly
   sliced
1 cup eggplant, peeled and
   diced
1 — 14½ oz. can stewed
   tomatoes
1 tsp. basil
½ tsp. oregano
½ tsp. thyme
¼ tsp. salt

SERVES 4
In a medium saucepan, saute onions, peppers and garlic in oil until tender. Stir in zucchini and eggplant and cook over low heat until eggplant is soft. Stir in remaining ingredients and simmer, uncovered, about 15 minutes.

MUSHROOMS FLORENTINE

2 — 10 pkg. frozen
   chopped spinach
½ tsp. salt
¼ cup chopped onion
2 Tbsp. butter, melted
½ cup grated Cheddar
   cheese
1 lb. fresh mushrooms
4 Tbsp. butter
¼ tsp. garlic powder
½ cup grated Cheddar
   cheese

SERVES 6
Cook spinach in boiling salted water. Drain well, squeezing out excess liquid. Spoon evenly into bottom of an 8 x 8 inch square baking dish. Sprinkle with salt; layer onion, melted butter and cheese over spinach.

Rinse and dry mushrooms. Slice and saute in 4 tablespoons butter. Spoon mushrooms over cheese layer and sprinkle with garlic powder. Top with grated Cheddar cheese. Bake at 350° 20-25 minutes until bubbly.

This side dish is delicious with a steak dinner…a good family-style vegetable dish.

CALIFORNIA MUSHROOMS

½ green pepper, finely
  chopped
½ cup chopped onion
2 cloves garlic, minced
⅓ cup olive oil
1 — 12 oz. can Italian
  tomatoes, chopped
1 tsp. garlic salt
3 Tbsp. grated Romano
  cheese
3 lb. fresh mushrooms
  (halved if big)
Salt and pepper to taste

SERVES 4-6

Saute green pepper, onion, and garlic in olive oil. Add cut-up tomatoes. Stir in garlic salt, cheese, and mushrooms. Salt and pepper to taste. Simmer, covered, for 15 minutes, then remove lid and simmer for 10 more minutes.

This old family recipe is a wonderfully different way to serve mushrooms.

STUFFED SWEET ONIONS

4 sweet white onions
  (Vidalia are the best)
1 cup frozen green peas,
  thawed
⅔ cup sliced fresh
  mushrooms
⅛ tsp. dried thyme
Dash of pepper
2 Tbsp. butter or margarine
¼ cup boiling water
½ tsp. chicken-flavored
  bouillon granules

SERVES 4

Cut a slice from the top of each onion, and scoop out centers, leaving ¼-inch thick shells. Save centers for something else. Place shells in a lightly greased 8-inch square baking dish.

Combine peas, mushrooms, thyme, and pepper; spoon evenly into onions, and dot with butter. Combine water and bouillon granules; pour over stuffed onions. Microwave for 7-9 minutes on high. Let stand 3 minutes before serving.

This unusual vegetable dish is so delicious and easy. It is sure to become a favorite!

VEGETABLES, RICE & PASTA

YOU'LL LOVE THESE NEW POTATOES

6 slices bacon, cut into
 ½ inch pieces
1½ lbs. small, new
 potatoes (about 24)
12 pearl onions, peeled
¾ cup chicken broth
½ lb. fresh mushrooms,
 sliced
¼ tsp. salt
¼ tsp. pepper
¼ cup minced fresh
 parsley

SERVES 6

Peel a small ring around the center of each potato. Cook bacon in a large skillet until transparent. Remove bacon from skillet, reserving 3 tablespoons of drippings. Add potatoes and onions to skillet and cook on high heat until lightly browned. Drain excess bacon drippings. Add chicken broth. Bring to a boil; cover, reduce heat and simmer 10 minutes or until potatoes are tender. Add mushrooms, and cook, uncovered, over high heat, stirring constantly, until liquid evaporates. Stir in bacon, salt, pepper, and parsley.

Southern cooking lives on!

NEW POTATOES WITH SNOW PEAS

14 small new potatoes
4 Tbsp. butter
½ tsp. salt
1 tsp. sugar
2 tsp. minced fresh parsley
2 cups fresh snow peas
 (can substitute frozen)
1-2 Tbsp. cooking oil

SERVES 6

Scrub new potatoes and place unpeeled potatoes in boiling water. Cook until just tender. In a small pan, melt butter, add salt, sugar, and parsley.

In a skillet, heat the oil, and add washed snow peas. Saute for 2 minutes. Add the potatoes and toss gently. Place in a serving dish and pour butter mixture over all.

VEGETABLES, RICE & PASTA

NEW POTATOES WITH BASIL

2 lbs. new potatoes,
    unpeeled and sliced
2 Tbsp. dry white wine
2 Tbsp. finely chopped
    green onion
1½ cups whipping cream
2 tsp. dried basil
¼ tsp. salt
¼ tsp. pepper
1 heaping tsp. cornstarch
    mixed with ¼ cup milk

SERVES 8

Cook potatoes in boiling salted water 10-15 minutes. Drain carefully, leaving skins intact. Keep potatoes warm.

Combine wine and green onions in a large saucepan. Bring to a boil and cook 1 minute. Add whipping cream; return to a boil. Reduce heat and simmer 20 minutes, stirring occasionally. Stir in basil, salt and pepper. Add cornstarch mixture to thicken, if desired.

Arrange potatoes on a serving plate; spoon sauce over potatoes. Serve immediately.

EASY POTATOES AU GRATIN

8 medium baking potatoes
2 cups shredded sharp
    Cheddar cheese
2 cups whipping cream
1½ tsp. salt
¼ cup soft bread crumbs
1 Tbsp. butter, melted

SERVES 8

Peel potatoes and parboil until soft enough to slice (about 10 minutes.) Alternate two layers of sliced potatoes and cheese in a lightly greased 2½ quart casserole. Combine whipping cream and salt; pour over potatoes. Sprinkle with bread crumbs and drizzle with butter. Cover and bake at 350° for 30 minutes. Remove lid and bake an additional 15 minutes.

177

VEGETABLES, RICE & PASTA

GOLDEN POTATO SURPRISE

6 large potatoes
6 slices bacon, cut in ½
  inch pieces
½ cup butter
2 cups shredded Cheddar
  cheese
2 cups sour cream
⅓ cup chopped green
  onion and tops
1 tsp. salt
¼ tsp. pepper
2 Tbsp. butter

SERVES 10
Boil potatoes in skin. Peel and grate. Fry bacon until crisp. Drain. Combine butter and cheese and cook over low heat until almost melted. Cool. Blend in sour cream, onions, salt, pepper and bacon. Stir lightly into potatoes. Place in greased 9 x 13 inch baking dish. Dot with butter. Bake at 350° for 40 minutes.

PRAIRIE SCHOONERS

4 large baked potatoes
1 — 15 oz. can ranch style
  beans
1 cup sour cream
1 stick butter, softened
Salt, pepper, and chili
  powder to taste
2 Tbsp. chopped green
  pepper
2 Tbsp. chopped onion
1 Tbsp. butter or margarine
1 cup Cheddar cheese,
  grated

SERVES 4
Slice off top one-third of baked potato lengthwise. Scoop out potato leaving ¼ inch around potato skin. Mash potato until free of lumps. Drain beans thoroughly, reserving juice. Mash beans. Whip sour cream, butter, mashed beans, salt, pepper, and chili powder. Add to mashed potatoes, adding enough bean juice to moisten. Spoon mixture into potato shells. Saute green pepper and onion in margarine. Top each potato with grated cheese, onion, and green pepper. Bake at 425° about 10 minutes or until browned.

OVEN-CRISPED POTATO SKINS

4 large baking potatoes,
  scrubbed well
Salt
Pepper
¼ cup butter or margarine,
  melted
Grated Cheddar cheese
Bacon, fried and crumbled
Chives, minced
Sour cream

SERVES 4
Bake potatoes in 375° oven until done. Cool slightly. Cut in half lengthwise, then again to make 4 quarters of each potato. Scoop out insides, leaving a little clinging to the skin. (Save the insides for mashed potatoes, potato soup or whatever.) Place peels on a buttered cookie sheet. Salt and pepper, then drizzle with butter. If desired, sprinkle with grated cheese and crumbled bacon. Bake at 425° for about 10 minutes or until crispy. Serve as is, or with sour cream and chives. These make a great side dish, snack or appetizer.

OVEN FRIES

3 medium unpeeled baking
  potatoes
2 tsp. vegetable oil
½ tsp. seasoning salt
⅛ tsp. pepper
Vegetable cooking spray

SERVES 6
Scrub potatoes, cut into strips. Place in a bowl and cover with cold water. Let stand 30 minutes; drain. Pat dry with paper towels.

Combine oil, salt, and pepper in a large plastic zip-lock type bag. Add potatoes, and toss well to coat. Arrange in a single layer on a baking sheet which has been coated with cooking spray. Bake at 475° for 25 minutes or until tender and browned, turning potatoes after 15 minutes.

VEGETABLES, RICE & PASTA

THANKSGIVING YAMS

2 — 40 oz. cans yams,
  drained
¼ cup brandy
⅔ cup fresh orange juice
1 Tbsp. grated orange rind
1 tsp. salt
½ cup brown sugar
½ tsp. ginger
¼ tsp. pepper
3 egg yolks

TOPPING:
⅔ cup brown sugar
1½ cups chopped pecans
½ tsp. cinnamon
½ cup butter, melted

SERVES 12
Mash yams until smooth. Add brandy, orange juice, rind, salt, sugar, ginger, pepper, and egg yolks. Beat to blend. Spoon into a buttered 9 x 13 inch baking dish. Mix topping ingredients thoroughly. Spread evenly over yams. Bake at 350° for 45-50 minutes, or until brown and bubbly.

This dish makes the perfect accompaniment to a Thanksgiving turkey.

SKILLET SQUASH

2 Tbsp. olive oil
1 large zucchini
1 large yellow summer
  squash
⅓ cup red bell pepper,
  chopped
½ tsp. oregano
½ tsp. salt
¼ tsp. black pepper
¼ tsp. garlic powder

SERVES 4
Slice squash into 1-inch chunks. Heat olive oil in medium skillet over medium heat. Add squash, pepper, and spices and saute for 10 minutes. Don't allow squash to become mushy.

This side dish is as tasty as it is pretty!

GARDEN ZUCCHINI

3-4 medium zucchini,
   quartered lengthwise
Garlic salt to taste
Freshly ground pepper
Oregano to taste
Basil to taste
½ cup sliced mushrooms
2-3 large fresh tomatoes,
   sliced ¼ inch thick
4-5 oz. Mozzarella cheese,
   sliced
2 medium onions, thinly
   sliced
4-5 bacon slices, cut up
2-3 Tbsp. Parmesan
   cheese, grated

SERVES 6-8

Place zucchini in a buttered, shallow baking dish. Season to taste with garlic salt, pepper, and herbs. Place mushrooms and tomatoes in a layer on zucchini. Season again. Layer cheese slices, then onions, then bacon on top of the zucchini. Sprinkle with Parmesan. Bake, uncovered at 350° for 45 minutes or until bubbly and zucchini is crisp-tender.

The bounty of your garden will make this outstanding zucchini dish a most popular summertime treat.

ROBIN'S ZUCCHINI RINGS

2 large (12-inch or longer)
   yellow or zucchini
   squash
2-3 small (5-inch) squash
   (2 green and 1 yellow)
3 beaten eggs
2 cloves garlic, minced
½ — 4 oz. can chopped
   green chilies
¾ cup chopped tomatoes
¼ tsp. black pepper
¼ tsp. oregano
½ tsp. parsley
¼ tsp. dill
¾ cup sour cream
½ lb. sliced Provolone
   cheese

SERVES 6

Using the large squash, slice 1½-inch slices of the neck portion of the squash. Using a knife, cut out the pulp. Set aside the rings and discard the pulp and body of the squash.

Dice the small squash, leaving the skin on. In a bowl combine, eggs, spices, herbs, tomato and zucchini, and mix thoroughly. Arrange rings in a greased baking dish. Fill rings with zucchini mixture. Top each ring with a dollop of sour cream. Place a generous slice of Provolone on top. Bake, uncovered, at 350° for 45 minutes.

VEGETABLES, RICE & PASTA

SOUTHWEST VEGETABLES

2 cups diced cooked
   vegetables (frozen
   mixed vegetables)
1 — 4 oz. can chopped
   green chilies
Butter, salt, pepper to taste

BATTER:
3 Tbsp. melted butter
3 eggs
1 egg yolk
1½ cups milk
¾ cup flour
1 tsp. sugar
½ tsp. salt
½ tsp. pepper

SERVES 6

Mix vegetables, chilies, salt, pepper and butter. Place batter ingredients in food processor or blender. Blend well and place half the batter in a 3-quart buttered casserole. Cover with vegetables and add remaining batter. Bake at 350° for 45 minutes or until browned and puffed.

This is a delicious vegetable dish. You may use any number of vegetable combinations with this recipe such as green beans and sauteed mushrooms, peas and carrots, corn and lima beans, or a combination of squashes. This goes well with any entree, but is particularly good with beef.

HARVEST VEGETABLE STIR FRY

2 Tbsp. vegetable oil
2 cups broccoli flowerets
2 cups cauliflowerets
2 cups fresh mushrooms,
   sliced
1 green pepper, sliced thin
1 cup celery, thinly sliced
1 cup carrots, thinly sliced
1 large clove garlic, peeled
   and minced
1 tsp. salt
1 tsp. pepper
2 Tbsp. soy sauce
½ cup Cheddar cheese,
   grated

SERVES 6-8

Heat oil to medium in wok or large skillet. Add broccoli, cauliflower, mushrooms, green pepper, celery, and carrots in that order. Saute. Add garlic, salt and pepper. Cover and cook 5 minutes until tender-crisp. Add soy sauce and toss to coat. Sprinkle cheese over all and cook until melted. Serve immediately.

To make this a main dish, add thin strips of cooked boneless chicken breast to the vegetables. Serve with rice for a delicious and easy meal.

RICE-STUFFED TOMATOES

10 small fresh tomatoes
Salt
2¼ cups quick-cooking
   brown rice, uncooked
1 cup chopped onion
2 Tbsp. olive oil
½ cup chopped walnuts,
   toasted
3 Tbsp. chopped fresh
   parsley
½ tsp. salt
¼ tsp. pepper
2 Tbsp. olive oil
¼ cup dry white wine
Fresh parsley sprigs

SERVES 10
Slice top off each tomato; set tops aside. Scoop out pulp. Sprinkle inside of each tomato shell with a pinch of salt, and invert on paper towels to drain.

Cook rice according to package directions, omitting salt and fat. Saute onion in 3 tablespoons oil until tender. Combine rice, onion, walnuts, parsley, salt and pepper. Spoon rice mixture into tomato shells; place on lightly greased 8 x 12 inch baking dish. Combine olive oil and wine; spoon over tomatoes. Cover and bake at 350° for 25 minutes. Place tomato tops on each stuffed tomato, and bake an additional 5 minutes. Garnish if desired.

NUTTY RICE PILAF

¼ cup vegetable oil
¾ cup pecans, chopped
1 cup celery, sliced
½ cup onion, chopped
1 tsp. salt
½ tsp. pepper
¼ tsp. thyme
1½ cups long grain white
   rice, uncooked
2½ cups hot chicken broth

SERVES 6
Heat oil in a large saucepan. Saute pecans, celery and onions until onion is transparent. Add seasonings and rice. Mix well. Cook 5 minutes; add chicken stock. Cover pan. Simmer until rice is tender and all liquid is absorbed, about 30 minutes.

A nice variation that goes well with beef.

VEGETABLES, RICE & PASTA

STEWED TOMATOES AND RICE

1 small zucchini, thinly
   sliced
½ cup chopped onions
2 Tbsp. butter
1 — 14½ oz. can stewed
   tomatoes, drained
1 cup long grain rice
1 cup water
1 tsp. chicken bouillon
   granules
¼ tsp. pepper

SERVES 6

In a saucepan, saute zucchini and onions in butter until zucchini is crisp-tender. Stir in remaining ingredients. Simmer, covered tightly, 25 minutes or until liquid is absorbed.

SPICY RICE

1 stick margarine
1 large onion, chopped
1 bell pepper, sliced thin
1 rib celery, sliced thin
1 large carrot, sliced thin
1 small jalapeno pepper,
   minced
1 — 10 oz. can beef
   consomme
1 soup can water
½ tsp. salt
¼ tsp. pepper
1 cup raw rice

SERVES 6

In a skillet, melt margarine and saute vegetables until limp. Add soup, water, salt, pepper, and rice. Transfer to a 1½-quart shallow casserole dish, and bake, covered, at 350° for 1 hour or until liquid is absorbed.

A great dish to serve with pork or chicken.

184

PASTA ON THE SIDE

1 — 8 oz. pkg. fettuccine
noodles
1 tsp. garlic salt
1 cup cream
½ cup Romano cheese
2 Tbsp. butter

SERVES 6
Cook noodles in boiling salted water for about 10 minutes. Add garlic salt, cream, cheese, and butter and cook until thickened.

This recipe is great for people on the go. Add anything you like to this from shellfish to veggies, or eat plain if you choose.

TWO-PEPPER FETTUCCINE

3 Tbsp. butter or margarine
1 small onion, finely
chopped
1 red pepper, diced
1 yellow pepper, diced
¾ cup chicken broth
½ tsp. salt
¼ tsp. black pepper
12 oz. fettuccine
Basil leaves
Parmesan cheese

SERVES 6
Melt 2 tablespoons butter in a skillet over low heat. Stir in onion; cover and cook for 5 minutes. Increase heat to medium; stir in red and yellow peppers. Cover again; cook for 10 minutes or until peppers are softened, stirring occasionally. Add broth, salt, and pepper. Bring to a boil; cook for 1 minute. Remove from heat; stir in remaining butter. Cover to keep warm.

Cook pasta in boiling salted water. Drain; place in a large serving bowl. Add pepper mixture; toss until well combined. Add basil; toss again. Serve with Parmesan.

VEGETABLES, RICE & PASTA

SEEDED FETTUCCINE

1 — 8 oz. pkg. fettuccine
  noodles
¾ cup cream
¼ cup butter or margarine
¾ cup sunflower kernels
⅓ cup grated Parmesan
  cheese
2 Tbsp. chopped parsley

SERVES 6

Cook noodles in boiling salted water until done. Drain. Stir in cream and butter. Toss in seeds, cheese, and parsley. Serve immediately.

The sunflower nuts give this recipe a unique flavor and texture…it is delicious with pork chops or chicken.

PASTA AND BROCCOLI

1 lb. fresh broccoli
¼ cup olive oil
2 cloves garlic, halved
1 Tbsp. minced fresh
  parsley
½ tsp. salt
¼ tsp. pepper
1 — 12 oz. pkg. fettuccine,
  cooked al dente and
  drained
½ cup Parmesan cheese

SERVES 4-6

Cut flowerets off broccoli stems; chop stems. Cook broccoli in boiling, salted water until tender, about 10 minutes. Drain well. In a large skillet, heat olive oil and saute garlic until golden. Discard garlic. Add broccoli, parsley, salt and pepper. Saute for 2 minutes. In a heated serving dish, toss warm pasta with broccoli mixture. Sprinkle with Parmesan and serve immediately.

The flavors in this recipe are so wonderful. It is easy to prepare and goes well with beef or pork. Try adding sliced, cooked, smoked sausage to this dish to make it a main course.

GARDEN ZUCCHINI LINGUINE

2 Tbsp. butter or margarine
1 Tbsp. olive oil
3 cloves garlic, minced
   or ¾ tsp. garlic powder
1 medium red onion, diced
4 small zucchini, thinly
   sliced
¾ tsp. dried thyme
½ tsp. salt
½ tsp. crushed red pepper
½ lb. linguine or fettuccine
½ cup grated Parmesan

SERVES 4

Melt butter with oil in skillet over medium high heat. Add garlic and onion and saute until lightly browned. Reduce heat and stir in zucchini, thyme, salt and crushed pepper. Continue stirring until zucchini is golden, but not limp.

Meanwhile, cook pasta according to package directions. Drain, reserving some liquid. Place in a large serving bowl, add zucchini mixture and Parmesan. Toss until well combined. May need to stir in some reserved liquid to moisten. Serve with additional Parmesan.

This is an easy side dish that goes well with most any entree. Use plain noodles if you don't have linguine or fettuccine.

DESSERTS

DESARTS

DUTCH APPLE CAKE

2 cups flour
3 tsp. baking powder
¾ cup sugar
1 tsp. salt
1 tsp. cinnamon
1 egg, beaten
¾ cup milk
⅓ cup shortening, melted
1½ cups apples, chopped

TOPPING:
½ cup sugar
3 Tbsp. flour
2 Tbsp. butter, softened
½ tsp. cinnamon

SERVES 10

Mix first five ingredients. Set aside. Combine egg and milk. Add shortening and blend. Add egg mixture to dry ingredients. Fold in apples and mix thoroughly. Turn into a greased 8-inch baking pan. Combine topping ingredients and sprinkle over batter. Bake at 400° for 25-30 minutes.

This is delicious as a dessert with vanilla ice cream or whipped cream to top it off. Also makes a terrific coffee cake.

ANGEL FOOD CAKE WITH CHOCOLATE WHIPPED CREAM

1 purchased angel food
   cake
1 cup powdered sugar
½ cup cocoa
¼ cup milk
⅛ tsp. cream of tartar
2 cups whipping cream

Mix powdered sugar, cocoa, milk and cream of tartar in a large bowl, blending until smooth. Cover and re-frigerate at least 1 hour.

With an electric mixer, gradually beat cream into chocolate mixture. Continue beating until stiff peaks form. Spread liberally on top and sides of angel food cake. Slice to serve.

This makes a beautiful cake, easy to make and most delicious!

LORRAINE'S BLACK WALNUT RING CAKE

½ cup golden raisins
1½ cups water
1½ tsp. baking soda
3 eggs
2 cups sugar
1 cup vegetable oil
3 cups flour
Dash salt
1½ tsp. baking powder
1 cup black walnut pieces

Combine raisins, water and soda in a saucepan. Heat to boiling. Set aside to cool. Combine eggs, sugar, and oil in a large bowl. Beat to blend. Sift together flour, salt, and baking powder. Add to egg mixture along with raisin mixture and juice. Beat well. Add nuts. Pour into well-greased tube pan. Bake at 325° for 60 to 70 minutes or until cake tests done.

This cake improves if baked a day before serving...it is a really good cake!

KIOWA CAKE

3 cups sugar
3 sticks butter
6 oz. cream cheese
6 eggs
2 heaping Tbsp. sour
  cream
3 cups flour
1 pkg. Dream Whip

SERVES 12
Cream together the sugar, butter, and cream cheese until light and fluffy. Add eggs one at a time, beating after each addition. Slowly mix in sour cream, flour, and Dream Whip. Beat 2-3 minutes. Pour into greased Bundt pan, and bake at 325° for 1½ hours.

If you are not counting calories, add this delicious cake to your "must try" list!

DESERTS

MARINAN'S BUTTERMILK CAKE

1 cup butter
2 cups sugar
4 eggs
1 Tbsp. vanilla
2 cups flour
½ tsp. soda
½ tsp. baking powder
Pinch of salt
1 cup buttermilk
1 cup heavy cream
2½ Tbsp. sugar
Fresh strawberries

Cream butter and sugar until light and fluffy. Add eggs one at a time, then vanilla, and mix well. Alternate dry ingredients with buttermilk, mixing well. Pour into a greased and floured tube pan and bake at 350° for 45 minutes. Heat cream and sugar, but do not let boil. Pour over cake when you take it out of the oven. Cool. Serve each slice with fresh strawberries on the side.

This old farm girl recipe is obviously loaded with calories, but is so easy and good, we had to include it!

CREME DE MENTHE CAKE

1 box white cake mix
4 large eggs
1 — 3½ oz. pkg. instant vanilla pudding mix
½ cup orange juice
¼ cup water
½ cup vegetable oil
¼ cup creme de menthe liqueur
¼ tsp. vanilla
1 — 5½ oz. can chocolate syrup

Grease and flour Bundt or tube pan. Combine all ingredients in mixer bowl except chocolate syrup. Beat about 4 minutes. Pour ⅔ of the batter into prepared pan. Add chocolate syrup to the remaining ⅓ batter and mix well. Pour over batter in pan. Do not mix. Bake 40-50 minutes at 350°. Remove from pan when cool. Dust with powdered sugar.

This cake is really rich, but a nice treat for company.

TOASTED BUTTER PECAN CAKE

2 cups pecans, chopped
¼ cup butter, melted
1 cup butter
2 cups sugar
4 unbeaten eggs
3 cups flour
2 tsp. baking powder
½ tsp. salt
1 cup milk
2 tsp. vanilla

BUTTER PECAN FROSTING:
¼ cup butter
1 lb. sifted powdered sugar
1 tsp. vanilla
4-6 tsp. evaporated milk or cream
Remaining pecans

SERVES 12

Stir together pecans and melted butter on a cookie sheet. Toast in 350° oven for 20-25 minutes, stirring frequently.

Cream 1 cup butter and sugar, blending well. Add eggs, mixing well. Sift together the flour, baking powder and salt, and add alternately with milk, beginning and ending with dry ingredients. Stir in vanilla and 1⅓ cups pecans. Turn into 3 greased and floured 9 inch cake pans, or a 9 x 13 inch pan. Bake at 350° for 25-30 minutes. Cool and spread frosting between layers and on top.

To make frosting, cream butter, sugar and vanilla. Add milk to reach desired spreading consistency. Stir in remaining ⅔ cup pecans.

ONE-STEP CHOCOLATE CAKE

1 pkg. devil's food cake mix
1½ cups sour cream
¾ cup vegetable oil
½ cup coffee liqueur or brewed coffee
2 eggs, beaten
1 — 4 oz. pkg. instant chocolate pudding
Powdered sugar

SERVES 8

Using an electric mixer or food processor, blend all ingredients except powdered sugar until smooth. Pour into greased 12-cup Bundt pan. Bake at 350° for 45 minutes or until it tests done. Cool. Invert onto serving platter and dust with powdered sugar.

This easy cake is not only delicious, but pretty enough to serve last minute company.

DESERTS

OATMEAL CAKE

1 cup quick oatmeal
1½ cups boiling water
1 cup white sugar
1 cup brown sugar
½ cup shortening
2 eggs
1 tsp. vanilla
1 tsp. salt
1 tsp. soda
1½ cups flour

FROSTING:
6 Tbsp. butter
⅔ cup brown sugar
¼ cup milk or cream
1 cup coconut
1 cup pecans, chopped
   (optional)

SERVES 12
Mix the oatmeal and water and let cool. Combine the sugars and shortening, add the eggs, then the remaining ingredients. Add the oatmeal mixture and blend well. Place in a 9 x 13 inch pan. Bake at 350° for 35-40 minutes. Frost while cake is warm.

Combine frosting ingredients in a saucepan. Boil for 2 minutes and spread on warm cake.

HEATH BAR CAKE

1 box German chocolate
   cake mix
1 — 14 oz. can sweetened
   condensed milk
1 — 12 oz. jar caramel ice
   cream topping
1 — 8 oz. carton Cool Whip
2-4 Heath Bars, crushed

SERVES 12
Bake cake according to directions in a 9 x 13 inch pan. Mix sweetened condensed milk and ice cream topping together. When cake is cooled, poke holes in it with a utility fork. Pour milk/topping mixture over top. Let set before frosting with Cool Whip. Sprinkle crushed Heath Bars on top. Keep refrigerated.

DESSERTS

HUMMINGBIRD CAKE

3 cups flour
1 tsp. soda
1 tsp. cinnamon
2 cups sugar
1 tsp. salt
1 cup oil
3 eggs, beaten
2 cups chopped bananas
  (4 medium bananas)
1½ cups chopped pecans
1 — 8 oz. can crushed
  pineapple
1 tsp. vanilla

**CREAM CHEESE
FROSTING:**
1 stick butter or margarine
1 — 8 oz. pkg. cream
  cheese, softened
1 tsp. vanilla
1 lb. powdered sugar
Milk

SERVES 12-15

In a large mixing bowl, combine first five ingredients. Add oil and eggs and stir just until dry ingredients are moistened. Stir in bananas, pecans, pineapple and vanilla. Pour batter into a greased and floured 9 x 13 inch pan. Bake at 350° for 30-35 minutes or until cake tests done. Cool before frosting with Cream Cheese Frosting.

To make frosting, combine cream cheese, butter, powdered sugar and vanilla. Beat until light and fluffy. Add milk to thin if necessary.

CRAZY POPCORN CAKE

1 cup unpopped popcorn
½ lb. miniature gum drops
1 lb. cashew nuts
1 lb. miniature
  marshmallows
½ cup oil
½ cup butter

Butter a large angel food cake pan. Put about ½ cup gum drops on the bottom of the pan. Pop popcorn. Put in a large bowl and add gum drops and cashew nuts, mixing together. In a saucepan, melt marshmallows, oil and butter. Pour over popcorn mixture and mix well. Press mixture tightly into prepared pan. Turn upside down onto serving plate. Cake is finished!

This is a wonderful treat for kids' parties, school occasions, or holiday times.

195

DESSERTS

SAM HOUSTON LEMON CAKE

¾ cup butter or margarine,
  softened
2 cups sugar
6 eggs
3 cups sifted flour
3 tsp. baking powder
¼ tsp. salt
½ tsp. lemon extract
1½ cups milk

LEMON FILLING:
2 eggs
1 cup sugar
1 Tbsp. butter or margarine
Rind of 1 lemon, grated
Juice of 2 lemons (¼ cup)
  (fresh is best)

SERVES 12-16
Grease and flour three 8-inch cake pans. (A 9 x 13 inch pan will work if you're not into layered cakes.)

Cream butter and sugar until smooth and creamy. Separate egg yolks from whites, beating yolks one at a time into creamed mixture. Beat hard after each addition.

Sift together flour, baking powder and salt. Stir lemon extract into milk and mix liquid alternately with dry ingredients into creamed mixture. Beat egg whites until they hold a point and fold into batter until blended. Pour into cake pans and bake for 35 minutes at 375° or until cake pulls away from sides of pans. Let cool. Spread a thin coating of lemon filling between each layer and over the top. (If baked in a 9 x 13 inch pan, spread lemon filling on top.)

To make lemon filling, beat eggs slightly in a saucepan. Stir in sugar, butter, lemon rind and juice and cook over low heat, stirring constantly until filling is thick enough to coat a spoon. Cool.

This light, refreshing cake was Sam Houston's favorite type dessert.

ORANGE CAKE

1 cup sugar
⅓ cup butter or margarine
2 eggs
1 tsp. vanilla
2 tsp. grated orange rind
1 cup buttermilk
1 tsp. baking soda
½ tsp. salt
1¾ cups flour

ORANGE FROSTING:
6 Tbsp. butter
Juice of 1 orange
Grated rind of 1 orange
3 cups powdered sugar

SERVES 12
Combine all ingredients in a bowl and mix well. Can also do easily in a food processor. Pour batter into a greased and floured 9 x 13 inch pan and bake at 350° for 40-45 minutes. Frost when cooled with Orange Frosting.

In a food processor, whip butter until softened. Add other ingredients and beat until spreading consistency. Spread on cooled cake.

POPPY SEED CAKE

1 butter recipe cake mix
   (or yellow pudding cake
   mix)
¾ cup sugar
¾ cup oil
4 eggs
8 oz. sour cream
2 Tbsp. poppy seeds
½ cup chopped pecans

GLAZE:
½ cup powdered sugar
Lemon juice (enough to
   make a thin glaze)

SERVES 12-15
Mix together all ingredients except pecans. Beat well for 2 minutes. Grease a Bundt or tube pan; line bottom with chopped pecans. Add batter and bake at 350° for 50 minutes or until cake tests done. Glaze while warm.

DESSERTS

PINEAPPLE PECAN CAKE

2 cups flour
2 cups sugar
2 eggs
1 tsp. vanilla
½ tsp. salt
2 tsp. baking soda
1 cup pecans, chopped
1 — 20 oz. can crushed
   pineapple, drained
1 Tbsp. vanilla

ICING I:
1 stick butter, softened
1 — 8 oz. pkg. cream
   cheese, softened
2 cups powdered sugar
1 tsp. vanilla
2 Tbsp. milk

ICING II:
1½ cups sugar
1 — 5 oz. can evaporated
   milk
1 stick margarine
1 cup coconut
1 cup chopped pecans

SERVES 12-15
Grease and flour a 9 x 13 inch pan. Put all ingredients for cake in a mixing bowl and mix well. Pour into prepared pan. Bake 35-40 minutes at 350°.

Icing I: Cream butter and cream cheese. Add sugar, vanilla, and milk. Frost while cake is hot. Refrigerate until time to serve.

Icing II: Boil sugar, milk, and margarine for 5-10 minutes until it starts to thicken. Remove from heat and add coconut and pecans. Pour over hot cake. Return to oven for 5 minutes.

Both of these icings are so good, we wanted to include them for you to choose. This is a delicious, easy cake that you'll love to serve.

VICKY'S RED VELVET CAKE

1 cup Crisco
1½ cups sugar
2 eggs
2 oz. red food coloring
2 Tbsp. cocoa
1 tsp. salt
1 cup buttermilk
2½ cups sifted flour
1 tsp. vanilla
1 Tbsp. vinegar
1 tsp. soda

FROSTING:
5 Tbsp. flour
1 cup milk
1 cup sugar
1 tsp. vanilla
1 cup Crisco

SERVES 12-15

Cream shortening, sugar, and eggs in a bowl. In a smaller bowl, make a paste with food color and cocoa. Add to creamed mixture and blend well. Add salt. Alternately add buttermilk with flour. Add vanilla; then stir in vinegar and soda. Do not beat hard. Pour into two greased and floured 9 inch cake pans. Bake in 350° oven 25-30 minutes or until cake tests done.

To make frosting, cook flour and milk in a saucepan over medium heat until thick (like mashed potatoes). Chill. Cream sugar, Crisco, and vanilla until fluffy. Mix together on medium speed until smooth. Spread on completely cooled cake and enjoy.

Vicky says her grandmother made this cake just for her when she came to visit...now her kids expect it at Christmas. Just another one of those "keepsake" recipes!

NO-BAKE CHOCOLATE COOKIES

2 cups sugar
½ cup evaporated milk
½ cup peanut butter
½ cup butter
4 Tbsp. cocoa
1 tsp. vanilla
3 cups oats

MAKES 3-4 DOZEN

Melt first four ingredients in a saucepan on medium heat. Add cocoa and cook to 240° on the candy thermometer (the soft ball stage). Remove from heat and add the vanilla and oats. Drop by spoonfuls onto waxed paper.

These are almost like a candy so kids really go for them. Most adults can't pass them up either!

DESERTS

FRESH APPLE COOKIES

½ cup shortening
1⅓ cups firmly packed
   brown sugar
1 egg
¼ cup milk
2 cups flour
1 tsp. baking soda
½ tsp. salt
1 tsp. cinnamon
½ tsp. nutmeg
1 cup raisins
1 cup chopped pecans
1 cup finely chopped,
   unpeeled Granny Smith
   apples

VANILLA FROSTING:
1½ cups sifted powdered
   sugar
⅛ tsp. salt
2½ Tbsp. milk
1 Tbsp. butter or
   margarine, melted
½ tsp. vanilla

MAKES 4½ DOZEN
Cream shortening and sugar, beating well. Add egg and milk; beat well. Combine dry ingredients and add to creamed mixture, mixing well. Stir in raisins, pecans, and apple.

Drop dough by teaspoonfuls onto greased cookie sheets. Bake at 400° for 12-15 minutes. Cool. Frost with vanilla frosting.

To make frosting, combine all ingredients in a small bowl; beat until smooth. Frost cookies.
What a delicious fall treat!

MRS. JOHNSON'S AFTER SCHOOL COOKIES

½ cup shortening
½ cup brown sugar
½ cup white sugar
1 egg, beaten
1 Tbsp. water
¾ cup flour
½ tsp. soda
½ tsp. salt
1½ cups rolled oats
1¼ cups chocolate chips

MAKES 3-4 DOZEN
Cream shortening and sugars. Add egg and water. Mix dry ingredients and stir into batter. Stir in chocolate chips. Drop by the spoonful onto a greased cookie sheet. Bake at 375° for 10-15 minutes.

CARAMEL COCONUT COOKIES

½ cup butter
½ cup brown sugar, firmly
  packed
1 cup flour

TOPPING:
1 cup brown sugar, firmly
  packed
2 eggs, beaten
½ tsp. salt
½ tsp. vanilla
2 Tbsp. flour
2 cups coconut
1 cup chopped nuts

MAKES 40 BARS
Mix butter, brown sugar, and flour. Press into a lightly greased 8 x 11 inch pan. Bake at 350° for 15 minutes.

Meanwhile, mix topping ingredients. Pour over baked crust. Bake at 350° for 15 minutes. Cool and cut into bars.

CHOCOLATE CHIP OATMEAL COOKIES

½ cup Crisco
½ cup butter or margarine
¾ cup sugar
¾ cup firmly packed brown
  sugar
2 eggs
1 — 3.4 oz. pkg. vanilla
  instant pudding mix
1 Tbsp. vanilla
1 tsp. baking soda
1 tsp. water
½ tsp. salt
1 cup oats
2¼ cups flour
1 — 12 oz. pkg. chocolate
  chips
1 cup chopped pecans
  (optional)

MAKES 2½ DOZEN
Beat shortening and butter until light. Add sugars and mix until fluffy. Add eggs, beating well. Add pudding mix, vanilla, soda, water and salt. Stir well. Mix in oats and flour until well blended. Stir in chocolate chips and nuts.

Drop by large teaspoonfuls onto a lightly greased cookie sheet, spacing about 2 inches apart. Bake at 375° for about 12 minutes or until cookies are lightly browned.

This variation on the traditional chocolate chip cookie is delicious…makes a wonderfully tender, moist cookie. Be sure to store in an airtight container.

DESSERTS

MRS. GRAHAM'S CHRISTMAS COOKIES

2½ cups flour
1 tsp. soda
1 tsp. salt
1 tsp. cinnamon
1 cup butter
1½ cups sugar
2 eggs
2 lbs. dates, chopped
½ lb. green and red
  candied cherries,
  chopped
½ lb. crystallized
  pineapple, cut up
1 lb. pecans, chopped

MAKES 8-10 DOZEN

Sift flour, soda, salt and cinnamon together in a large bowl. Cream butter and sugar. Add eggs and beat until smooth. Blend in flour mixture. Add dates, candied fruits and nuts. Mix well. Drop by teaspoonful on ungreased cookie sheet. Bake at 400° for 10 minutes. Do not overcook.

These delicious holiday cookies come to us by way of Mississippi from one of the best cooks in the South!

LEMON NUT COOKIES

¾ cup butter, softened
½ cup brown sugar, firmly
  packed
¼ cup sugar
1 egg
1 Tbsp. lemon juice
1½ cups flour
¾ tsp. baking soda
½ tsp. salt
1 — 10 oz. pkg. white
  chocolate chips
1 cup pecans, chopped
2 tsp. grated lemon peel

MAKES 2-3 DOZEN COOKIES

Beat butter and sugars until creamy. Beat in egg and lemon juice. Gradually blend in flour, baking soda, and salt. Stir in white chocolate chips, pecans and lemon peel. Drop by heaping teaspoonfuls onto ungreased cookie sheets. Bake 7-10 minutes at 375° or until lightly browned. Remove from sheet and cool.

BLUE RIBBON CHOCOLATE COOKIES

½ cup shortening
1 cup sugar
1 egg
2 squares unsweetened
   chocolate, melted
¾ cup buttermilk
1 tsp. vanilla
1¾ cups flour
½ tsp. soda
½ tsp. salt
1 cup nuts, chopped
12 large marshmallows,
   halved

CHOCOLATE FROSTING:
2 Tbsp. margarine, melted
¼ cup cocoa
⅛ tsp. salt
3 Tbsp. milk
¾ tsp. vanilla
1¾ cups powdered sugar

MAKES 2 DOZEN
Cream shortening and sugar. Add egg, chocolate, buttermilk, and vanilla. Stir in dry ingredients and mix well. Chill for 1 hour. Roll into balls the size of a walnut and bake on a lightly greased cookie sheet at 350° for 6-8 minutes. Just before they are done, put ½ large marshmallow on top and return to oven until marshmallow is puffy. Cool and frost with Chocolate Frosting. Sprinkle with chopped nuts if desired.

These cookies won Grand Champion at the El Paso County Fair...they'll be winners at your house, too!

CHOCOLATE CHEWIES

1¼ cups margarine,
   softened
2 cups sugar
2 large eggs
2 tsp. vanilla
2 cups flour
¾ cup cocoa
1 tsp. baking soda
Powdered sugar

MAKES 5 DOZEN
Cream margarine and sugar. Add eggs and vanilla. Beat well. Gradually blend in dry ingredients into creamed mixture. Drop by teaspoon onto ungreased cookie sheet. Bake at 350° for 9-11 minutes. Transfer cookies to a waxed paper sheet and sprinkle with powdered sugar when completely cooled. Store in an airtight container.

DESSERTS

CHOCOLATE MINT SUGAR COOKIES

1 cup sugar
¾ cup vegetable oil
2 eggs
1 tsp. vanilla
2½ cups flour
1½ tsp. baking powder
¾ tsp. salt
¾ cup mint chocolate
   chips
Sugar

MAKES 3 DOZEN

In a large bowl, combine sugar and oil and mix well. Beat in eggs and vanilla. Stir in dry ingredients and mix well. Stir in mint chips. Shape into 1 inch balls and roll in sugar. Place on ungreased cookie sheet. Bake at 350° for 8-10 minutes.

EASIEST COOKIES OF ALL

½ cup butter, softened
1 can Eagle Brand milk
7 oz. flaked coconut
1 cup pecans, chopped
2 lbs. powdered sugar

MAKES 3-4 DOZEN

Blend butter and Eagle Brand well. Stir in coconut and pecans. Add powdered sugar and mix well. Roll into small balls and chill.

These are great for kids to make at Christmas.

GINGERSNAPS

¾ cup soft shortening
1 cup brown sugar, firmly
   packed
1 egg, unbeaten
¼ cup molasses
2 cups sifted flour
¼ tsp. salt
2 tsp. soda
1 tsp. ginger
1 tsp. cinnamon
1 tsp. cloves
Sugar

MAKES 4 DOZEN

Combine shortening, sugar and egg in mixing bowl and beat until fluffy. Add molasses and beat well. Sift dry ingredients together and add. Mix well. Chill dough thoroughly; shape into 1 inch balls and roll in granulated sugar. Place 2 inch apart on greased baking sheets. Bake at 350° for 12-15 minutes.

MEXICAN WEDDING COOKIES

½ lb. butter
5 Tbsp. sugar
2 tsp. vanilla
2 cups sifted flour
2 cups finely chopped
   pecans
Powdered sugar

MAKES 30 COOKIES
Mix first five ingredients in order given. Roll into small balls. Place on a greased baking sheet. Bake at 325° for 25 minutes. Roll in powdered sugar when cooled.

RAISIN BRAN NUT COOKIES

½ cup firmly packed brown
   sugar
¼ cup oil
2 Tbsp. water
2 egg whites, slightly
   beaten
1 tsp. cinnamon
½ tsp. baking soda
⅛ tsp. salt
1 cup flour
1½ cups raisin bran cereal
¼ cup pecans, chopped

MAKES 4 DOZEN
Mix sugar, oil, water, egg whites, cinnamon, baking soda and salt in a large bowl. Stir in flour and cereal. Mix in nuts. Drop by rounded teaspoons onto lightly greased baking sheets. Bake at 350° for 10 minutes or until lightly browned.

This low-fat cookie is an excellent choice for those on low cholesterol diets.

SHORTBREAD COOKIES

1 lb. butter, softened
1½ cups powdered sugar
3 cups flour
½ cup cornstarch

MAKES 4 DOZEN
Cream butter and sugar until light and fluffy. Add flour and cornstarch and beat well for 8-10 minutes. Roll dough into balls the size of walnuts, place on an ungreased cookie sheet, and press with a fork to make a crisscross pattern on top. Bake at 325° for 18-20 minutes.

These wonderfully rich cookies just melt in your mouth.

DESSERTS

PECAN PIE SURPRISE BARS

1 pkg. yellow cake mix
½ cup butter or margarine,
   melted
1 egg

FILLING:
⅔ cup reserved cake mix
½ cup firmly packed brown
   sugar
1½ cups dark corn syrup
3 eggs
1 tsp. vanilla
1 cup chopped pecans

MAKES 30 BARS
Generously grease bottom and sides of 9 x 13 inch baking pan. Reserve ⅔ cup dry cake mix for filling. In large mixing bowl, combine remaining dry cake mix, butter, and egg. Mix until crumbly. Press into prepared pan. Bake at 350° for 15 minutes or until lightly browned. Meanwhile prepare filling by mixing reserved cake mix, brown sugar, corn syrup, eggs, and vanilla. Pour over partially baked crust. Sprinkle with pecans. Return to oven and bake 30-35 minutes or until filling is set. Cool and cut into bars.

PECAN SANDIES

1 cup butter or margarine,
   softened
1 cup white sugar
1 cup brown sugar
2 eggs
1 tsp. vanilla
1 cup oil
1 tsp. soda
1 tsp. cream of tartar
½ tsp. salt
4¼ cups flour
1 cup finely chopped
   pecans

MAKES 4-6 DOZEN
Combine butter and sugars, beating until light and fluffy. Add eggs, vanilla, and oil, blending well. Combine dry ingredients and stir into mixture. Dough will be stiff. Drop by teaspoonful onto lightly greased cookie sheets. Bake at 350° for 20 minutes or until lightly browned.

These light, fluffy cookies are simply divine!

DESSERTS

SCOTCHEROOS

1 cup white Karo syrup
1 cup white sugar
1 cup creamy peanut butter
6 cups Rice Krispies
1 — 6 oz. pkg. chocolate
  chips
1 — 6 oz. pkg. butterscotch
  chips

MAKES 2-3 DOZEN
Combine Karo and sugar in a small saucepan. Bring to just boiling. Stir in peanut butter. Pour over cereal and mix well. Press into a greased 9 x 13 inch pan. Melt together the chocolate and butterscotch chips. Spread on top of cereal mixture. Cool slightly and cut while soft.

These quick, delicious cookies are great to make ahead, easy to carry to picnics or pack in lunches. Keep tightly covered.

BEST EVER SOFT SUGAR COOKIES

2 sticks margarine
2 cups sugar
3 eggs
1 tsp. vanilla
2½ cups flour
⅛ tsp. salt
3 tsp. baking powder

**POWDERED SUGAR
FROSTING:**
1 Tbsp. butter, melted
1½ cups powdered sugar
Milk
1 tsp. vanilla

MAKES 2½ DOZEN
Cream together the margarine and sugar. Add eggs one at a time and beat to blend; stir in vanilla. Add flour, salt, and baking powder and mix until well blended. Roll into balls the size of walnuts and place on an ungreased cookie sheet. Flatten with the bottom of a glass. Bake at 350° just until edges are browned. Do Not Overbake. Frost with powdered sugar frosting, tinted appropriately for the season.

To make frosting, add powdered sugar to butter and mix. Add milk gradually to reach the right consistency for frosting. Stir in vanilla.

DESSERTS

WHEATIES COOKIES

½ cup margarine
½ cup shortening
1 cup brown sugar
1 cup white sugar
2 eggs, beaten
½ tsp. vanilla
1 tsp. soda
½ tsp. baking powder
½ tsp. salt
1 cup coconut
2 cups flour
3 cups Wheaties cereal

MAKES 3-4 DOZEN
Cream together margarine, shortening, and sugars. Add eggs and vanilla. Mix dry ingredients, then add gradually to the butter/sugar mixture. Roll into small balls and bake at 350° for about 12 minutes.

NO-BAKE CANDY BAR COOKIES

1½ cups chocolate chips
1 cup butterscotch chips
1 cup peanut butter
1 lb. powdered sugar
½ cup margarine
¼ cup milk
2 Tbsp. dry instant vanilla
   pudding
1½ cups dry roasted
   peanuts

MAKES 36 BARS
Line a 9 x 13 inch pan with waxed paper. Melt chocolate and butterscotch chips. Add peanut butter and mix well. Pour ½ of this mixture into prepared pan. Spread thinly. Refrigerate until set.

Beat sugar, margarine, milk and dry pudding together until blended. Spread on chocolate layer. Refrigerate 10 minutes. Add peanuts to remaining chocolate mixture and spread evenly over sugar layer. Refrigerate 2 hours or overnight. Cut into 1 inch squares. Store in refrigerator.

DESSERTS

DOUBLE CHOCOLATE BROWNIES

2 squares unsweetened
   chocolate
¼ cup butter
2 eggs
1 tsp. vanilla
1 cup sugar
½ cup flour
1 cup chocolate chips

MAKES 1 DOZEN

Melt chocolate squares and butter together in a small saucepan over low heat. Set aside. In a bowl, beat eggs, adding sugar gradually to blend; stir in vanilla. Add melted chocolate mixture and beat. Stir in flour and chips. Pour into greased and floured 8 inch pan. Bake at 350° for 30 minutes.

Yummy!

CHEESE CRUNCHERS

1 — 12 oz. pkg.
   butterscotch chips
6 Tbsp. butter
2 cups graham cracker
   crumbs
2 cups chopped nuts
2 — 8 oz. pkg. cream
   cheese, softened
1 cup sugar
4 eggs
¼ cup flour
2 Tbsp. lemon juice

MAKES 2 DOZEN BARS

Melt butterscotch chips and butter over low heat. Fold in graham cracker crumbs and nuts. Mix well. Reserve 2 cups for topping. Press remainder in a 9 x 13 inch baking dish. Bake at 350° for 12 minutes. Cool.

Combine cream cheese and sugar. Beat until creamy. Add eggs one at a time, blending well. Mix in flour and lemon juice. Pour evenly over baked crust. Sprinkle reserved crumbs on top. Bake at 350° for 25 minutes. Chill before serving.

DESSERTS

LEMON CRUNCH BARS

1⅓ cups soda crackers,
    finely rolled
¾ cup butter or margarine
½ cup sugar
¾ cup flour
½ cup coconut
1 tsp. baking powder
3 eggs, beaten
1 cup sugar
1 lemon, rind and juice
¼ cup butter or margarine

MAKES 16

Crumble crackers, butter, sugar, flour, coconut, and baking powder together. Remove 1 cup of crumbs for topping. Press remaining crumbs into greased 9 x 9 inch pan. Bake at 350° for 15 minutes. Remove from oven.

In a small saucepan, beat eggs together with sugar, lemon juice and rind, and butter. Heat over medium heat, stirring, until thickened. Spread over crumb crust. Sprinkle reserved crumbs over top. Return to oven and finish baking until lightly browned. Cool and cut into squares.

PAYDAY BARS

1 cup sugar
1 cup white Karo syrup
1 cup creamy peanut butter
1 tsp. vanilla
6 cups chex cereal
1 cup Spanish peanuts

MAKES 2 DOZEN BARS

Mix sugar and Karo in a small saucepan. Cook over medium heat, stirring constantly until boiling. Stir in peanut butter and vanilla. In a bowl, mix together the cereal and peanuts. Pour hot mixture over and stir to blend. Press into a lightly greased 9 x 13 inch pan. Cut into bars to serve.

DESSERTS

CHOCOLATE-PEANUT BUTTER BROWNIES

⅓ cup butter or margarine,
   softened
½ cup peanut butter
½ cup sugar
½ cup brown sugar, firmly
   packed
2 eggs
1 cup flour
1 tsp. baking powder
¼ tsp. salt
1 tsp. vanilla
1 — 6 oz. pkg. chocolate
   chips

MAKES 18 BROWNIES
Cream butter and peanut butter. Gradually add sugars, beating well. Add eggs, one at a time, beating well after each addition. Stir in dry ingredients and blend well. Add vanilla and chocolate chips.

Pour batter into a greased 8-inch baking pan. Bake at 350° for 30-35 minutes. Cool and cut into squares.

Try these easy treats next time you have to bring cookies to a meeting or school party.

JUST PEACHY OATMEAL BARS

¾ cup butter or margarine
1¼ cups rolled oats
1¼ cups flour
½ cup sugar
1½ tsp. baking powder
1 cup peach preserves
   (apricot is good, too)
1 cup coconut

MAKES 2½ DOZEN
Melt margarine in a small bowl in microwave. Stir in rolled oats, flour, sugar, and baking powder until blended. Mixture will be crumbly; reserve ½ cup crumbs. Pat remaining mixture in bottom of 9 x 13 inch pan. Spread preserves to within ½ inch of edges. Sprinkle on coconut and remaining crumbs. Bake at 350° for 25-30 minutes or until browned. Cool in pan. Cut into small squares.

DESSERTS

GRANDMA'S FUDGE OAT BARS

1 cup brown sugar
1 cup sugar
1 cup butter or margarine
2 eggs
2 cups flour
3 cups rolled oats
1 tsp. soda

FUDGE TOPPING:
1 cup chocolate chips
½ cup margarine
1 tsp. vanilla
1 — 14 oz. can Eagle Brand
   milk

MAKES 2-3 DOZEN
Cream sugars and butter, adding eggs one at a time. Combine dry ingredients together. Blend with creamed mixture. Put ⅔ of this into a 9 x 13 inch pan.

To make topping, melt chocolate chips together with margarine in microwave or in a small saucepan over low heat. Add vanilla and Eagle Brand and stir to blend. Pour on top of crust. Cover with remaining ⅓ oat mixture. Bake at 350° for 30 minutes. Don't cut until cool.

TURTLE BARS

2 cups flour
¾ cup light brown sugar,
   packed
½ cup butter, softened
1½ cups pecan halves
½ cup light brown sugar,
   packed
⅔ cup butter
1½ cups milk chocolate
   chips

MAKES 3-4 DOZEN
Mix flour, brown sugar, and butter in a food processor or with a mixer, until mixture is crumbly. Press into a 9 x 13 inch greased pan. Cover crust with rows of pecan halves.

In a saucepan, stir together brown sugar and butter until mixture bubbles. Boil for ½ to 1 minute. Pour over crust. Bake 18-22 minutes at 350° until caramel bubbles and browns. Remove from oven and sprinkle with milk chocolate pieces. Let stand for 3 minutes for chocolate to melt, then swirl chocolate. Cut in squares while warm. Delicious!

PEANUT BUTTER AND FUDGE BARS

CHOCOLATE PORTION:
2 cups sugar
1 cup margarine, or butter, softened
4 eggs
2 tsp. vanilla
1½ cups flour
¾ cup cocoa
1 tsp. baking powder
½ tsp. salt
1 cup chocolate chips

PEANUT BUTTER PORTION:
¾ cup peanut butter
⅓ cup margarine or butter, softened
⅓ cup sugar
2 Tbsp. flour
¾ tsp. vanilla
2 eggs

FROSTING:
3 squares unsweetened chocolate
3 Tbsp. margarine or butter
2⅔ cups powdered sugar
¼ tsp. salt
¾ tsp. vanilla
4-5 Tbsp. water

MAKES 36 BARS

In a large bowl, cream sugar and butter until light. Add eggs, beating well. Stir in vanilla. Gradually add dry ingredients, blending well. Stir in chocolate chips.

In a smaller bowl, blend peanut butter and margarine until smooth. Add sugar and flour, blend well. Add vanilla and eggs, beat until smooth.

Spread half of the chocolate mixture in a greased 9 x 13 inch pan. Spread peanut butter mixture evenly over chocolate mixture. Spread remaining chocolate mixture evenly over peanut butter mixture. Pull a knife through layers in wide curves, marbling the mixtures.

Bake at 350° 40-45 minutes. Cool.

To make frosting, melt chocolate and margarine over low heat, stirring constantly until smooth. Remove from heat, stir in sugar, salt, vanilla, and water to make desired spreading consistency. Frost cooked brownies. Cut into bars.

DESSERTS

OATMEAL PEAR SQUARES

2 cups flour
1 cup quick cooking oats
1 cup flaked coconut
1 cup brown sugar, firmly
   packed
1 tsp. baking soda
¼ tsp. salt
1 cup butter
4 medium pears, peeled,
   cored and chopped (can
   use canned)
½ cup chopped nuts
¼ cup sugar
¼ tsp. cinnamon
¼ tsp. ginger
3 Tbsp. butter

MAKES 2½ DOZEN BARS

In a large bowl, stir together flour, oats, coconut, brown sugar, baking soda and salt. Cut in 1 cup butter until mixture is crumbly. Press half mixture into a greased 9 x 13 inch pan. Cover with pears. Combine nuts, sugar, and spices and sprinkle over fruit. Dot with 3 tablespoons butter. Pat remaining oat mixture over all. Bake at 375° for 45-50 minutes. Cool and cut into squares.

Try these for a welcome spicy treat on a cold winter afternoon. Good and good for you!

RICE KRISPIE BARS

¼ cup butter or margarine
45 regular marshmallows,
   or 4½ cups miniature
   marshmallows
6 cups Rice Krispies

MAKES 32 BARS

Melt butter or margarine in a 3 quart saucepan over low heat. Add marshmallows and cook, stirring continuously until marshmallows are melted. Remove from heat and add cereal, stirring to coat. Press warm mixture evenly into a buttered 9 x 13 inch pan. Cool and cut into bars.

We love this all-time favorite and wanted to include it as we find ourselves hunting this recipe on various boxes, wrappers, etc. Now it is a part of our permanent record!

RASPBERRY BARS

½ cup butter or margarine
2 cups vanilla chips, or
   2 — 6 oz. white baking
   bars, chopped
2 eggs
½ cup sugar
1 cup flour
½ tsp. salt
1 tsp. amaretto liqueur or
   almond extract
½ cup raspberry
   spreadable jam
¼ cup sliced almonds,
   toasted

MAKES 2 DOZEN

Melt butter over low heat. Remove from heat and add 1 cup of vanilla chips. Let stand; do not stir.

In large bowl, beat eggs until foamy. Gradually add sugar, beating at high speed until lemon colored. Stir in butter/chip mixture. Add flour, salt, and amaretto; mix at low speed until just combined. Spread ½ batter in greased and floured 9 inch square pan. Bake at 325° for 15-20 minutes.

Stir remaining 1 cup vanilla chips into remaining batter; set aside. Melt jam. Spread evenly over warm, partially baked crust. Gently spoon remaining batter over fruit spread. Sprinkle with almonds. Bake at 325° an additional 25-35 minutes. Cool completely. Cut into bars.

This rich cookie is too good to be true!

DESSERTS

ROCKY ROAD SQUARES

1 pkg. devil's food cake
mix
½ cup margarine or butter,
melted
¼ cup brown sugar, firmly
packed
⅓ cup water
2 eggs
1 cup chopped nuts
2 cups miniature
marshmallows
1½ cups chocolate chips

MAKES 36 SQUARES

Mix half the dry cake mix, margarine, brown sugar, water and eggs in a large bowl until smooth. Stir in remaining cake mix and 1 cup nuts. Spread in greased and floured 9 x 13 inch pan and bake at 350° for 20 minutes. Sprinkle marshmallows evenly over top and return to oven for about 5 minutes or until the marshmallows are puffed and golden brown.

Melt chocolate chips in microwave or in a saucepan over low heat. Drizzle over top of browned marshmallows. Cool completely.

For high altitude, stir 2 tablespoons flour into dry cake mix and bake at 375°.

TEMPTING TREATS

1½ cups chocolate-
covered graham cracker
crumbs (about 17
crackers)
3 Tbsp. margarine, melted
1 — 8 oz. pkg. cream
cheese, softened
½ cup chunky peanut
butter
1 cup powdered sugar
¼ cup chocolate chips
1 tsp. shortening

MAKES 1 DOZEN

Stir together crumbs and margarine in a small bowl. Press into a 9-inch square baking pan. Bake at 350° for 10 minutes. Cool.

Beat cream cheese, peanut butter and sugar in a small bowl until well blended. Spread over crust.

Melt chocolate chips with shortening over low heat. Drizzle over cream cheese layer. Chill 6 hours or overnight.

216

APRICOT TARTS

1 — 6 oz. pkg. dried
  apricots
1½ Tbsp. sugar
½ cup water
2 sticks margarine
1 — 8 oz. pkg. cream
  cheese
2 cups flour
⅛ tsp. salt
Powdered sugar

MAKES 12-18 TARTS

Chop apricots into small pieces. Place in a saucepan with sugar and ½ cup water. Cook over medium heat until apricots are tender. Remove from heat and cool.

Mix softened margarine and cream cheese until well blended. Add flour and salt and mix to form dough. Roll out as a pie crust; cut into 3-inch rounds. Fill each round with 1 teaspoon apricots. Fold over and seal with fork. Bake 24 minutes at 350° or until lightly browned. Sprinkle with powdered sugar when cool.

GRAHAM CRACKER CRUST

1 cellophane wrapped pkg.
  graham crackers (about
  20 crackers)
¼ cup sugar
⅓ cup butter, softened

MAKES ONE 9-INCH CRUST

Crush graham crackers in a food processor, or place in a plastic bag and crush them with a rolling pin. They should be finely crushed. Combine crumbs, sugar and butter and blend well. Press crumb mixture into 9-inch pie plate, covering the bottom and sides evenly. Bake at 375° for 8 minutes and cool.

DESSERTS

FLAKY PIE CRUST

PER CRUST:
1⅓ cups flour
½ tsp. salt
½ cup Crisco
About 3-4 Tbsp. ice water

MAKES ONE 9-INCH CRUST

Mix flour and salt with one hand. Add Crisco and break up shortening in flour until pieces are pea size. Sprinkle cold water over mixture and toss around with hand. Add enough water until dough holds together when gathered, as if making a snow-ball. Avoid working the dough too much.

To make dough in a food processor, combine flour, salt and Crisco in processor. Blend until mealy. Add ice water, a tablespoon at a time with machine running, until dough makes a ball.

Flatten dough on floured surface and roll about an inch larger than pan. Put in pan and trim edges. For a baked pie shell, bake at 450° for 8-10 minutes. (Be sure to prick the bottom and sides.)

SOUTHERN CHESS PIE

1¼ cups sugar
½ cup butter, melted
3 well-beaten eggs
1 Tbsp. white vinegar
1 tsp. vanilla
1 — 9 inch unbaked pie
   shell

SERVES 6-8

Preheat oven to 400°. Mix all ingredients together and beat well. Pour into uncooked pie shell. Bake for 10 minutes, then reduce temperature to 325°. Bake about 45 minutes more or until set.

DESSERTS

BANANA SPLIT PIE

CRUST:
2 cups graham cracker
  crumbs
½ cup butter or margarine,
  melted

FILLING:
1 cup butter or margarine,
  softened
2 eggs
2 cups powdered sugar
5-6 bananas, sliced and
  sprinkled with lemon
  juice
1 — 20 oz. can crushed
  pineapple, drained
1 — 8 oz. container Cool
  Whip
⅓ cup chopped nuts,
  optional
Maraschino cherries,
  optional

SERVES 12
Mix melted margarine and graham cracker crumbs. Press into a 9 x 13 inch pan. For filling, whip margarine, eggs, and powdered sugar until light and fluffy, about 10 minutes. Spread over graham cracker crust. Top with bananas, pineapple, whipped topping, nuts and cherries. Cover and refrigerate at least 4 hours before serving.

KEY LIME PIE

1 — 9 inch prepared
  graham cracker crust
4 egg yolks
1 — 14 oz. can sweetened
  condensed milk
3 oz. Key West lime juice

SERVES 6-8
Combine egg yolks and sweetened condensed milk and blend well. Add lime juice gradually and beat until filling is smooth and creamy. Pour into graham cracker crust and bake at 350° for 10 minutes. Chill. Can serve plain or with whipped cream.

This pie has just the right amount of tartness, and runs a close second to that delicious favorite you can only get in Florida!

DESSERTS

BLUEBERRY CREAM PIE

¾ cup sugar
¼ cup cornstarch
½ tsp. salt
2½ cups milk
3 egg yolks
1 Tbsp. butter or margarine
1 tsp. vanilla
2 cups fresh blueberries
 (or 1 — 16 oz. can
 drained)
1 — 9 inch pie shell, baked
1 cup whipping cream
¼ cup powdered sugar

SERVES 6-8

Combine sugar, cornstarch, salt, and milk in a heavy saucepan; stir well to remove lumps. Cook over medium heat, stirring constantly, until mixture thickens and boils. Cook 1 minute stirring constantly. Remove from heat.

Beat egg yolks until thick and lemon colored. Gradually stir about ¼ of hot mixture into yolks; add to remaining hot mixture, stirring constantly. Cook over medium heat 2 minutes, stirring constantly. Remove from heat; add butter and vanilla. Blend well. Gently stir in blueberries. Cool and pour into pie shell.

Beat whipping cream until foamy; gradually add powdered sugar, beating until soft peaks form. Spread over pie and chill.

MOM'S LEMON CHEESE PIE

1 — 9 inch prepared
 graham cracker crust
1 — 8 oz. pkg. cream
 cheese
2 cups cold milk
1 — 4 oz. pkg. lemon
 instant pudding

SERVES 6-8

Whip softened cream cheese with ½ cup milk, blending well. Mix remaining milk and pudding for 1 minute until thickened. Stir in cream cheese. Pour in graham cracker crust and refrigerate several hours.

Need a quick, delicious dessert? This one is the ticket!

DESSERTS

HEAVENLY CHOCOLATE PIE

CRUST:
4 egg whites
¼ tsp. cream of tartar
½ cup sugar
Another ½ cup sugar
¼ cup cocoa
½ cup chopped pecans
¼ tsp. vanilla

FILLING:
1 cup whipping cream
¼ cup sugar
½ tsp. cocoa
¼ tsp. instant coffee
½ tsp. vanilla

MAKES 1 9-INCH PIE

Beat egg whites and cream of tartar, gradually adding ½ cup sugar until stiff. Mix together the ½ cup sugar, cocoa, chopped pecans, and vanilla and fold into meringue mixture. Pour into a buttered 9-inch pie tin and bake at 325° for 35 minutes. Cool.

In a chilled bowl, whip the cream. Then add sugar, cocoa, instant coffee and vanilla, stirring to blend. Pour into cooled meringue crust. Refrigerate.

KENTUCKY BOURBON PIE

2 eggs slightly beaten
1 cup sugar
½ cup flour
½ cup butter, melted and cooled
1 cup chopped pecans
1 — 6 oz. pkg. chocolate chips
1 tsp. vanilla
1 — 9 inch pie shell, unbaked
1 cup whipping cream
1 Tbsp. bourbon
¼ cup powdered sugar

SERVES 6-8

Combine eggs, sugar, flour and butter in a bowl and beat until just blended. Stir in pecans, chocolate chips, and vanilla. Pour into pie shell and bake at 350° for 45-50 minutes.

Beat whipping cream and bourbon until foamy. Add powdered sugar gradually, beating until soft peaks form. Serve pie warm with whipped cream.

DESSERTS

LEMON SPONGE PIE

Juice and rind of 2 or 3
  lemons
1½ cups sugar
3 eggs, separated
⅛ tsp. salt
3¾ Tbsp. flour
1½ cups milk
1 — 9 inch unbaked pie
  shell

MAKES 1 9-INCH PIE
Mix together the juice, rind, sugar,
egg yolks, salt, flour, and milk. Fold
in stiffly beaten egg whites. Pour into
an unbaked pie shell and bake at
350° for 1 hour or until set.

*This recipe is very old, coming to us
from a wonderful family cook in Ohio.*

DOUBLE PUMPKIN PIE

4 oz. cream cheese,
  softened
1 Tbsp. milk or half-and-
  half
1 Tbsp. sugar
1½ cups Cool Whip
1 prepared graham cracker
  crust
2 — 3.5 oz. pkg. vanilla
  instant pudding
1 cup cold milk
1 — 16 oz. can pumpkin
1 tsp. cinnamon
½ tsp. ginger
¼ tsp. cloves

SERVES 8
Mix cream cheese, milk and sugar
in a large bowl with a wire whisk
until smooth. Gently fold in whipped
topping. Spread on bottom of crust.

Mix pudding mix and milk, beating
with a wire whisk until well blended.
Mixture will be thick. Stir in pumpkin
and spices with whisk, and mix well.
Spread over cream cheese layer.
Refrigerate at least 3 hours. Garnish
each slice with a dollop of Cool
Whip, if desired.

*This is a nice change from traditional
pumpkin pie, and so easy, too!*

DESSERTS

SUSAN'S BUTTERSCOTCH CREAM PIE

1 — 6 oz. pkg. butterscotch
    morsels
1 — 3¾ oz. pkg. instant
    vanilla pudding mix
1 cup sour cream
1 cup milk
1 prepared 9-inch
    chocolate cookie pie
    crust
1 cup heavy cream
1 Tbsp. powdered sugar
1 oz. unsweetened
    chocolate

MAKES 1 9-INCH PIE
Melt butterscotch morsels in microwave or over low heat and stir until smooth. In a bowl, combine pudding mix, sour cream and milk and beat well. Stir in butterscotch. Pour into pie crust and chill 1 hour.

Whip cream and powdered sugar to soft peaks. Spread over pie. Grate chocolate on top.

This pie is so rich and good...great to eat when you're wanting to splurge!

PECAN TASSIES

CREAM CHEESE PASTRY:
1 — 6 oz. pkg. cream
    cheese, chilled and
    cubed
1 cup butter or margarine,
    chilled and cubed
2 cups flour

FILLING:
½ cup butter
½ cup brown sugar
1 cup light corn syrup
1 tsp. vanilla
3 eggs
1 cup pecans, chopped

MAKES 4 DOZEN
In a food processor, combine cream cheese and butter until well blended. Add flour to make a dough. Chill. (Can also do this by hand or with a mixer.) Shape dough into 48 balls; place each ball into greased mini-muffin tins, and press to form a shell.

To make filling, combine butter and brown sugar until well blended. Gradually add corn syrup. Stir in vanilla and eggs. Mix well. Fold in pecans.

Fill each pastry shell ¾ full with mixture. Bake at 325 for 25-30 minutes. Remove immediately and cool on rack.

DESERTS

PEANUT BUTTER PIE

1 — 8 oz. pkg. cream
  cheese, softened
½ cup sugar
½ cup creamy peanut
  butter
1 tsp. vanilla
1 cup whipping cream
1 — 9 inch prepared
  graham cracker crust
1-2 Tbsp. chopped salted
  peanuts

SERVES 6-8
Combine cream cheese and sugar; beat until smooth. Add peanut butter and vanilla and beat well. Set aside. Beat whipping cream until soft peaks form; fold into peanut butter mixture. Spoon into crust. Sprinkle with chopped peanuts. Chill at least 3 hours before serving.

This is a deliciously rich pie...easy to prepare and a nice change of pace.

PEANUT BUTTER TEMPTATION

1 cup powdered sugar
½ cup creamy peanut
  butter
1 — 9 inch pie shell, baked
¼ cup cornstarch
⅔ cup sugar
¼ tsp. salt
2 cups milk, scalded
3 egg yolks, beaten
2 Tbsp. butter or margarine
¼ tsp. vanilla

MERINGUE:
3 egg whites, room
  temperature
6 Tbsp. sugar
¼ tsp. cream of tartar

SERVES 6-8
Combine powdered sugar and peanut butter. Mix well with fork until the mixture resembles coarse meal. Spread half the mixture in pie shell. Set remaining mixture aside.

Combine remaining ingredients in a saucepan. Cook over medium heat until thick, stirring constantly. Spoon filling over peanut butter layer in pastry shell.

To make meringue, beat egg whites until stiff, adding sugar and cream of tartar gradually to mixture. Spread over filling. Sprinkle remaining peanut butter mixture over meringue. Bake at 325° for 20 minutes or until meringue is firm and lightly browned. Cool before serving.

PINEAPPLE PIE

1 — 14 oz. can sweetened
  condensed milk
½ cup lemon juice (fresh is
  best)
1 — 20 oz. can crushed
  pineapple, drained
1 — 8 oz. carton Cool Whip
1 — 9 inch prepared
  graham cracker crust

SERVES 6-8
Combine condensed milk and lemon juice. Stir well. Fold in pineapple and whipped topping. Spoon mixture into crust. Chill.

This is a nice, light pie…would make a wonderful summer dessert.

FRIED MINCE PIES

1 can refrigerator biscuits
Mincemeat or favorite pie
  filling
Powdered sugar

Roll biscuits into 4-inch circle. Place 1 tablespoon mincemeat on half of each biscuit; fold over. Seal the edges; prick tops. Fry in deep fat 365° about 8 minutes. Drain; roll in powdered sugar.

WORLD'S EASIEST PIE

2 — 6 oz. prepared graham
  cracker crusts
1 — 14 oz. Eagle Brand
  milk
1 — 20 oz. can crushed
  pineapple, drained
1 — 21 oz. can cherry pie
  filling
1 — 12. oz. carton Cool
  Whip

MAKES 2 PIES
Blend together the milk, pineapple, and cherry pie filling. Fold in Cool Whip until well blended. Spoon into prepared graham cracker crusts.

Chill at least 4 hours. Can be frozen.

Ever need a pie in a hurry? This one is the ticket, and it makes two to boot!

DESSERTS

BAKED ALASKA

1 — 10 inch prepared angel
    food cake
1 pint strawberry ice
    cream, softened
1 pint pistachio ice cream,
    softened
6 egg whites
½ tsp. cream of tartar
½ cup sugar

SERVES 12-15

Slice cake horizontally into 3 layers. Place one layer on freezer-to-oven serving plate. Spread strawberry ice cream over first layer. Top with second cake layer; spread pistachio ice cream over cake. Top with third cake layer; freeze until firm.

Beat egg whites (at room temperature) and cream of tartar until foamy. Gradually add sugar, 1 tablespoon at a time beating until stiff peaks form. Remove cake from freezer; quickly spread meringue over entire surface, making sure edges are sealed to plate. Bake at 500° for 2-3 minutes or until peaks are browned. Slice dessert and serve immediately.

APPLE KUCHEN

½ cup margarine
1 box yellow cake mix
½ cup flaked coconut
2½ cups peeled, thinly
    sliced baking apples
1 tsp. cinnamon
½ cup sugar
1 cup sour cream
1 egg

SERVES 12

Mix margarine and dry cake mix until crumbly; mix in coconut. Pat mixture into ungreased 9 x 13 inch pan, building up edges. Bake 10 minutes at 350°. Arrange apple slices on warm crust. Mix sugar and cinnamon and sprinkle on apples. Blend sour cream with egg. Drizzle over apples. Bake 25 minutes or until edges are light brown; do not overbake. Delicious hot or cold.

BLUEBERRY UPSIDE DOWN DESSERT

1 — 16 oz. can blueberry
   pie filling
⅔ cup brown sugar
⅓ cup butter or margarine
1¼ cups flour
¾ cup sugar
1½ tsp. baking powder
1 tsp. salt
¼ cup butter or margarine,
   melted
¾ tsp. vanilla
1 egg

SERVES 6
Pour can of blueberry pie filling in the bottom of a loaf pan. Combine brown sugar and butter and cream well. Spread over blueberries.

Mix remaining ingredients well and pour over blueberry mixture. Bake at 375° for 40 minutes. Serve hot with ice cream or whipped topping. Good cold too.

POLLY'S BERRIED DELIGHT

1½ cups crushed graham
   crackers
¼ cup sugar
⅓ cup margarine, melted
1 — 8 oz. pkg. cream
   cheese, softened
¼ cup sugar
2 Tbsp. milk
3½ cups Cool Whip
2 pints strawberries,
   halved
2 — 3.4 oz. pkgs. instant
   vanilla pudding
3½ cups cold milk

SERVES 12
Combine crumbs, ¼ cup sugar and melted margarine. Press into a 9 x 13 inch pan and chill. Beat softened cream cheese, ¼ cup sugar and 2 tablespoons milk until smooth. Fold in half of the Cool Whip and spread over crust. Spread strawberries over this, saving a few for garnish. Prepare pudding with 3½ cups cold milk. Pour over berries. Chill. Before serving, spread rest of Cool Whip on top and garnish with strawberries.

May use bananas, peaches or pineapple instead of strawberries. Great dessert for a group!

DESSERTS

SHARON'S CREAM PUFF DESSERT

1 stick margarine
1 cup water
1 cup flour
4 eggs
1 large box instant vanilla
   pudding
3 cups milk
1 — 8 oz. pkg. cream
   cheese, softened
1 — 8 oz. carton Cool Whip
Chocolate syrup

SERVES 12

Boil together the margarine and water. Add flour and mix well. Cool slightly and stir in eggs, 1 at a time. Mix well and spread into a 9 x 13 inch greased pan. Bake at 400° for 30 minutes. Cool completely.

In a large bowl, mix pudding, milk and cream cheese. Beat until lumps disappear. Pour into cream puff crust. Spread Cool Whip on top of pudding and drizzle syrup on top. Refrigerate. This keeps well for days.

GERMAN CHOCOLATE CHEESECAKE

CRUST:
1 pkg. German chocolate
   cake mix
½ cup shredded coconut
⅓ cup butter or margarine,
   softened
1 egg

FILLING:
16 oz. cream cheese
2 eggs
¾ cup sugar
2 tsp. vanilla

TOPPING:
2 cups sour cream
1 tsp. vanilla
¼ cup sugar

SERVES 8-10

Mix crust ingredients until crumbly. Press into ungreased 9 x 13 inch pan. Beat filling ingredients together until smooth and fluffy. Spread over crust. Bake at 350° for 25-30 minutes. Cool.

Combine topping ingredients and spread over cooled filling. Refrigerate for several hours before serving.

Another delicious choice for cheesecake fanatics!

DESSERTS

CHEESECAKE SQUARES

1 cup flour
⅓ cup firmly packed brown
   sugar
6 Tbsp. butter or
   margarine, softened
1 — 8 oz. pkg. cream
   cheese, softened
¼ cup sugar
1 egg
2 Tbsp. milk
1 Tbsp. lemon juice
½ tsp. vanilla
1 Tbsp. finely chopped
   pecans

MAKES 16 SQUARES

Combine flour and brown sugar; cut butter in until mixture resembles crumbs. Reserve 1 cup of crumb mixture. Press remaining mixture into an ungreased 8-inch square pan. Bake at 350° for 12-15 minutes or until lightly browned.

Beat cream cheese until light and fluffy. Gradually add sugar, mixing well. Add next 4 ingredients blending well. Spoon cream cheese mixture over crust. Combine reserved crumbs and pecans; sprinkle over cream cheese mixture. Bake at 350° for 25-30 minutes. Cool; cut into squares.

DESERTS

BLACK FOREST CHEESECAKE

1½ cups chocolate wafer
   crumbs
¼ cup butter or margarine,
   melted
3 — 8 oz. pkgs. cream
   cheese, softened
1½ cups sugar
4 eggs
⅓ cup kirsch, or other
   cherry-flavored liqueur
4 —1 oz. squares
   semisweet chocolate
½ cup sour cream
Whipped cream
Maraschino cherries with
   stems

SERVES 6-8

Combine chocolate crumbs and butter, mixing well. Firmly press into bottom and 1 inch up sides of a 9-inch springform pan.

Beat cream cheese until light and fluffy. Gradually add sugar mixing well. Add eggs, one at a time, beating well after each addition. Stir in kirsch, and mix until blended. Pour into prepared pan. Bake at 350° for 1 hour. Let cake cool on a wire rack.

Melt chocolate squares in microwave or double boiler. Cool slightly; stir in sour cream. Spread chocolate mixture evenly over top. Chill thoroughly. Garnish with whipped cream and cherries.

TALLEY'S CHERRY JUBILEE

½ lb. vanilla wafers,
   crushed
1 stick margarine
1½ cups powdered sugar
2 eggs
1 — 16 oz. can cherry pie
   filling
1 — 8 oz. carton Cool Whip

SERVES 8-10

Line a 9 x 13 inch pan with ⅔ of the crushed wafers. Cream margarine, powdered sugar and eggs until smooth. Spread over wafers. Spread cherry pie filling over creamed mixture. Top with Cool Whip, sprinkling remaining wafer crumbs on top. Put in freezer for 30 minutes to set. Keep in refrigerator.

We love to serve this dessert at family gatherings. It serves a crowd and is so easy.

DESSERTS

DIRT DESSERT

¼ cup butter or margarine,
  softened
1 cup powdered sugar
8 oz. cream cheese
2 — 3 oz. pkg. instant
  French vanilla pudding
3¼ cups milk
12 oz. extra creamy Cool
  Whip
20 oz. pkg. Oreo cookies

SERVES 8

Cream butter, sugar and cream cheese. In a separate bowl, beat instant pudding and milk together until smooth. Fold in Cool Whip and mix this into cream cheese mixture. Refrigerate. Crush cookies in a food processor (or place in plastic bag and crush with rolling pin) until they resemble fine sand.

In an 8 inch plastic flower pot, layer ⅓ cookie crumbs on bottom, ½ pudding, ⅓ cookies, ½ pudding, then ⅓ cookies. Refrigerate. (This can also just be layered in a glass salad bowl.)

Add silk flowers to this dessert to resemble a spring bouquet, and use as a centerpiece! Try making these in little individual plastic pots for each of your guests.

ICE CREAM CRUNCH

1½ cups flour
1 cup quick oatmeal
½ cup brown sugar
1½ cups chopped nuts
1 cup butter
1 — 6 oz. jar caramel
  topping
½ gallon vanilla ice cream

SERVES 10-12

Combine first five ingredients. Spread in a thin layer on a jelly roll pan. Bake at 350° for 30 minutes or until brown. Cool and crumble. Put half the crumbs in a 9 x 13 inch pan. Spoon caramel topping over crumbs. Spread softened ice cream over caramel. Top with remaining crumbs. Freeze. Cut in squares to serve.

DESESRTS

FROZEN RAINBOW DELIGHT

2 cups whipping cream
3 Tbsp. powdered sugar
18 soft macaroon cookies,
   crumbled
1 cup chopped pecans
1 tsp. vanilla
1 quart raspberry sherbet
1 quart lime sherbet
1 quart orange sherbet

SERVES 16

Beat whipping cream until foamy; gradually add sugar, beating until soft peaks form. Fold in macaroon crumbs, pecans, and vanilla.

Spread half of macaroon mixture in bottom of a two-piece 10-inch tube pan. Spread raspberry sherbet evenly over macaroon mixture; freeze 30 minutes. Repeat with other sherbets, freezing 30 minutes between layers. Top with remaining macaroon mixture, and freeze until firm.

Let frozen dessert stand at room temperature 10 minutes before serving. Remove side piece of tube pan; slice.

FROZEN OREO DESSERT

6 oz. chocolate chips
¾ cup white corn syrup
¼ cup evaporated milk
1 Tbsp. butter
¼ tsp. vanilla
20 Oreo cookies, crushed
⅓ cup butter, melted
½ gallon vanilla ice cream,
   softened
¼-½ cup chopped nuts

SERVES 12-15

Heat chips and syrup in a saucepan, stirring until smooth. Add milk, butter and vanilla. Cool. While mixture is cooling, crush Oreos in a zip-lock bag with a rolling pin. Mix with melted butter, and press into a 9 x 13 inch baking dish. Spread softened ice cream over Oreo layer. Pour cooled chocolate mixture over ice cream. Sprinkle chopped nuts on top. Freeze.

WILL'S ICE CREAM CAKE

1 pkg. Oreo cookies
⅓ cup butter, melted
⅓ cup slivered toasted
   almonds
2 pints softened coffee ice
   cream
1 pint softened vanilla ice
   cream
2 cups semi-sweet
   chocolate chips
¼ cup milk or cream
¼ cup Grand Marnier

SERVES 12
Crush cookies and mix 4 cups crumbs with melted butter and toasted almonds. Reserve a few almonds and a small amount of cookie crumbs for topping. Place crumb mixture in a 10-inch springform pan and pat. Bake at 375° for about 15 minutes or until mixture forms a crust. Cool.

Fill the crust with the ice cream, layering the flavors. Sprinkle top with the reserved crumbs and almonds and freeze solid.

Make a chocolate sauce by melting the chocolate chips over low heat. Add cream to thin, then stir in liqueur.

Serve cake with drizzled chocolate sauce over each slice.

ORANGE CHANTILLY

1⅓ cups whipping cream
1 cup powdered sugar
⅔ cup sour cream
3 Tbsp. Cointreau or other
   orange-flavored liqueur
½ tsp. grated orange rind
1 tsp. vanilla

MAKES 3 CUPS
Combine whipping cream and sugar in a chilled bowl. Beat at low speed until blended. Increase speed to high and beat until peaks begin to form.

Combine sour cream, liqueur, orange rind, and vanilla; fold gently into whipped cream just until blended. Serve in sherbet glasses with wafer cookies.

DESSERTS

PRESIDENT'S DAY DESSERT

1 — 16 oz. can cherry pie filling
1 — 16 oz. can crushed pineapple, drained
1 pkg. yellow or white cake mix
1 stick butter or margarine
1 cup chopped nuts

SERVES 10-12
Pour cherry pie filling and crushed pineapple into a 9 x 13 inch baking pan. Sprinkle dry cake mix over fruit. Dot with 1 stick butter or margarine. Top with 1 cup chopped nuts. Bake at 350° for 45 minutes.

It doesn't get any easier than this!

PETITE PINEAPPLE TORTES

3 eggs, separated
¾ cup sugar
1 cup crushed pineapple, drained
1 tsp. baking powder
¼ tsp. salt
1 cup graham cracker crumbs
½ cup finely chopped pecans

RUM SAUCE:
¼ cup honey
3 Tbsp. butter
Grated rind of 1 lemon
2 Tbsp. lemon juice
1 cup water
½ cup sugar
1 Tbsp. cornstarch
Dash of salt
2 Tbsp. dark rum

MAKES 1 DOZEN
Beat egg yolks and sugar until thick. Stir in pineapple. Mix together the baking powder, salt, crumbs, and nuts. Stir into the pineapple mixture. Beat the egg whites to stiff. Fold into pineapple/crumb mixture. Spoon batter into greased muffin cups and bake at 375° for 18-20 minutes. Serve with Rum Sauce over each torte.

To make Rum Sauce, combine honey, butter, lemon juice and rind, and water in a saucepan. Combine sugar, cornstarch, and salt; stir into honey mixture. Bring mixture to a boil, stirring constantly. Cook 5 minutes. Remove from heat and stir in rum. Good over ice cream, too.

RAISIN PUDDING DELIGHT

1 cup brown sugar
1 heaping Tbsp. butter
½ tsp. vanilla
½ cup raisins
2 cups water
1 Tbsp. butter or margarine
½ cup white sugar
1 cup flour
½ tsp. salt
2 tsp. baking powder
½ cup milk

SERVES 6

Combine first five ingredients in a saucepan. Bring to a boil and stir for 2 minutes. Remove from heat.

In a bowl, combine butter, sugar, flour, salt, baking powder and milk to make a batter.

Pour raisin mixture in a 2 quart baking dish. Add batter on top. Bake at 350° for 30 minutes.

This quick, easy dessert is a nice change of pace. Serve hot with ice cream or whipped cream.

APPLE FOLDOVERS

1 pkg. puff pastry shells
6 cups peeled, sliced
    apples
¾ cup firmly packed brown
    sugar
¾ cup chopped pecans
3 Tbsp. butter or
    margarine, melted
1½ Tbsp. lemon juice
2 tsp. cornstarch

GLAZE:
3 Tbsp. butter
1 cup powdered sugar
Milk

MAKES 12

Bake puff pastry shells according to package directions.

Combine apples, brown sugar, pecans, butter, lemon juice, and cornstarch in a medium saucepan, stirring until cornstarch dissolves; bring to a boil. Reduce heat to low; cook, uncovered about 10 minutes or until apples are tender. Spoon hot filling into pastry shells. Glaze while warm.

To make glaze, combine butter and powdered sugar in a small bowl. Add milk to make proper consistency.

DESERTS

OLD-FASHIONED STRUDEL

BISCUIT DOUGH:
2 cups flour
1½ tsp. baking powder
1 tsp. salt
¾ cup shortening
¼ cup milk

FILLING:
6 tart apples
1 cup stewed apricot
 pieces
1 cup raisins
1½ cups sugar
1 tsp. cinnamon
½ tsp. nutmeg
1 tsp. vanilla
1 stick butter

SERVES 12

Mix flour, baking powder, and salt. Cut in shortening until mixture is crumbly. Stir in milk until dough sticks together. Roll out and cut into strips and pieces. Arrange half the pieces in the bottom of a greased Dutch oven or 2½ inch deep baking pan. (Pieces should not touch.)

Peel and slice apples. Mix with apricots and raisins. Place over biscuit dough pieces. Mix sugar and spices and sprinkle over fruit. Put more biscuit dough pieces on top. Melt butter, add vanilla, and pour over top. Bake at 350° until apples are done, about 30-45 minutes.

We like to make this recipe at the chuckwagon when we brand. Using scraps left from sourdough biscuit dough, we cook this in a 12 inch Dutch oven. It is a wonderful dessert indoors or out...you will love its old-fashioned flavor and versatility.

236

STRAWBERRY PIZZA

1 — 20 oz. pkg. refrigerated
sugar cookie dough
1 — 8 oz. pkg. softened
cream cheese
1 — 14 oz. can sweetened
condensed milk
⅓ cup lemon juice
1 tsp. vanilla
½ cup sugar
2 Tbsp. cornstarch
½ cup water
1 pint fresh strawberries,
halved
Few drops red food
coloring

SERVES 8-10
Pat cookie dough out in a 14-inch pizza pan. Bake at 350° for 7-9 minutes or until golden brown. Cool.

Combine cream cheese, milk, lemon juice, and vanilla. Mix well and spread on cooled crust. Chill.

Combine sugar and cornstarch in a saucepan. Add water, mixing until smooth. Cook over medium heat until thickened, stirring constantly. Add strawberries and food coloring. Cool completely. Spread strawberry mixture over cream cheese layer. Chill. Cut in wedges to serve.

This dessert takes a little time as it is important to chill each layer, but it is well worth it!

DESERTS

TIGER BUTTER

1 lb. almond bark or white
    chocolate
½ cup peanut butter
    (creamy or crunchy)
½ cup chocolate chips

Melt almond bark and peanut butter in a saucepan over low heat or in the microwave. Stir to blend. Spread mixture on a foil-lined cookie sheet. Melt chocolate chips, then drizzle over peanut butter mixture. Swirl together. Chill and break into pieces to serve.

CRUNCHY CARAMEL BALLS

1 large pkg. jumbo
    marshmallows
1 — 12 oz. pkg. caramels
1 — 14 oz. can Eagle Brand
    milk
1 stick butter or margarine
Rice Krispies

MAKES 3 DOZEN
In a large saucepan over low heat, melt together the caramels, milk, and butter. Stir until creamy. Cool. Using tongs, dip each marshmallow in the caramel mixture, then roll in Rice Krispies. Set on waxed paper.

Kids think these are the greatest!

NEVER-FAIL FUDGE

1 large can evaporated
    milk
4½ cups sugar
⅓ cup butter
2 — 7 oz. Hershey bars
1 — 12 oz. pkg. milk
    chocolate chips
⅛ tsp. salt
2 tsp. vanilla
1 pint marshmallow creme

Boil milk, sugar, and butter on medium heat for 5 minutes. Remove from heat and add candy bars and chocolate chips, salt, vanilla, and marshmallow. Beat until candy is melted, and ingredients are well mixed. Add nuts and pour into greased 9 x 13 inch dish.

This is truly the best, most perfect fudge you'll find!

CHOCOLATE CHRISTMAS PIZZA

1 — 12 oz. pkg. semi-sweet
  chocolate chips
1 lb. white almond bark,
  divided
2 cups miniature
  marshmallows
1 cup crisped rice cereal
1 cup peanuts
1 — 6 oz. jar red
  maraschino cherries,
  drained and cut in half
3 Tbsp. green maraschino
  cherries, drained and
  quartered
⅓ cup coconut
1 tsp. oil

SERVES 10-12

Melt together the chocolate chips and 14 oz. of the almond bark. Stir until smooth. In a large bowl, combine marshmallows, cereal, and peanuts. Pour chocolate mixture over cereal mixture and blend. Pour onto greased 12-inch pizza pan. Top with cherries; sprinkle with coconut. Melt remaining 2 oz. almond bark with oil, stirring until smooth. Drizzle over coconut. Refrigerate until firm. Store at room temperature.

This colorful Christmas dessert is a hit with kids and adults alike. Makes a great gift, too!

GRANDMA'S BEST TREATS

1 stick margarine
1 — 12 oz. pkg. chocolate
  chips
1 — 12 oz. jar creamy
  peanut butter
1 — 12 oz. box Crispix
  cereal
Dry roasted peanuts,
  optional
2 cups powdered sugar

MAKES 12 CUPS

Melt margarine, chocolate chips, and creamy peanut butter together. Mix cereal and peanuts in a large bowl. Pour melted mixture over cereal mixture. Stir until well-coated. Put powdered sugar in a large plastic bag. Pour cereal mixture into bag and shake until well coated. Refrigerate in an airtight container.

These make a good school party snack or Christmas treat.

INDEX

INDEX

241

INDEX

INDEX

INDEX

INDEX

INDEX

INDEX

INDEX

INDEX

KITCHEN KEEPSAKES
39265 Rd. 45-49
Kiowa, CO 80117

☐ **KITCHEN KEEPSAKES**
☐ **MORE KITCHEN KEEPSAKES**
Please send me information on ☐ **KITCHEN KEEPSAKES**
BY REQUEST

Name_____

Address _____

City _____ State _____ Zip _____

KITCHEN KEEPSAKES
39265 Rd. 45-49
Kiowa, CO 80117

☐ **KITCHEN KEEPSAKES**
☐ **MORE KITCHEN KEEPSAKES**
Please send me information on ☐ **KITCHEN KEEPSAKES**
BY REQUEST

Name_____

Address _____

City _____ State _____ Zip _____

KITCHEN KEEPSAKES
39265 Rd. 45-49
Kiowa, CO 80117

☐ KITCHEN KEEPSAKES
☐ MORE KITCHEN KEEPSAKES
Please send me information on ☐ **KITCHEN KEEPSAKES**
BY REQUEST

Name_____

Address _____

City _____ State _____ Zip _____